Afterglow

A Test of Human Spirit

Jean Catherine Vaughn

BALBOA.
PRESS

A DIVISION OF HAY HOUSE

Balboa Press books may be ordered through booksellers or by contacting:

Balboa Press
A Division of Hay House
1663 Liberty Drive
Bloomington, IN 47403
www.balboapress.com
1-(877) 407-4847

Because of the dynamic nature of the Internet, any web addresses or links contained in this book may have changed since publication and may no longer be valid. The views expressed in this work are solely those of the author and do not necessarily reflect the views of the publisher, and the publisher hereby disclaims any responsibility for them.

The author of this book does not dispense medical advice or prescribe the use of any technique as a form of treatment for physical, emotional, or medical problems without the advice of a physician, either directly or indirectly. The intent of the author is only to offer information of a general nature to help you in your quest for emotional and spiritual well-being. In the event you use any of the information in this book for yourself, which is your constitutional right, the author and the publisher assume no responsibility for your actions.

Any people depicted in stock imagery provided by Thinkstock are models, and such images are being used for illustrative purposes only.
Certain stock imagery © Thinkstock.

Printed in the United States of America

ISBN: 978-1-4525-4986-6 (sc)
ISBN: 978-1-4525-4984-2 (hc)
ISBN: 978-1-4525-4985-9 (e)

Library of Congress Control Number: 2012906420

Balboa Press rev. date: 6/1/2012

This book is dedicated to my husband, Donald Ray Vaughn. He provides the stability that supports my growth in becoming a whole person. I love you.

Acknowledgments

I thank my wonderful family for tolerating the closed door of my office, the sign that I was writing and was not to be disturbed. I especially want to thank my husband, Don, who picked up the slack when I was entrenched in my fever for the story.

Gratitude is bestowed upon my sisters in Spirit, Susan Chartiers and Tricia Pritchard. Susan shared many of my spiritual journeys and became my database of memory when my recollection on a specific event was cloudy. Tricia is my personal editor and, like me, became consumed by the book. I would not have been able to come this far without her support and editing expertise.

A special thanks goes out to Emily Kotek and Amanda Lutz for creating proto-types for the cover and to my daughters-in-law, Cris and Saeunn, who worked together to fine tune the digital print that eventually became the cover. I would also like to thank Roy Bath for suggesting the wonderful quote by Albert Einstein.

Without the kindness of strangers, this book would not have come to fruition. The very first edit was done by a man named Stephen King, a friend of a friend whom I never met. He gave me the encouragement to proceed with the story. There were several book clubs and individuals who reviewed the book whom were unknown to me at the time. I thank them all for their participation in helping this book progress to publication.

The writing of our story was started one year after Melanie's death. I could not have finished it without the guidance of Great Spirit, Grandmother Twylah Hurd Nitsch, and Melanie's help from beyond.

With gratitude to one and all, I love you and thank you.

Certificate of Death Date: July 8, 2004

Time of Death: 12:15 AM

Date Pronounced Dead: July 2, 2004

Was Cased Referred to Medical Examiner/Corner: Yes

Immediate Cause of Death: Stab Wound to Abdomen

Was an Autopsy Performed: Yes

Were Autopsy Findings Available Prior to Completion of Cause of Death: Yes

Manner of Death: Suicide

Date of Injury: July 1, 2004

Time of Injury: 11:00 PM

Describe How Injury Occurred: Self-Inflicted Stab Wound

Location: Home–Harrisburg, PA

Date Filed: July 4, 2004

Afterglow

I'd like the memory of me to be a happy one. I'd like to leave an afterglow of smiles when life is done. I'd like to leave an echo whispering softly down the ways; of happy times and laughing times, of bright and sunny days. I'd like the tears of those who grieve to dry before the sun. Of happy memories I leave behind, when my day is done.

Anonymous

Chapter 1

I ask myself, "How can this be?" I sit in the front pew of Holy Rosary Catholic Church in Erie, Pennsylvania, apprehensively awaiting the start of the funeral mass for my youngest child. My husband is by my side; my children and their families surround me acting as the protective glue that keeps me cemented to my sanity.

This is the parish of my children's youth. Their religious and elementary school education took place on this block nestled within a working class neighborhood of tree-lined boulevards and older city homes. As I observe the familiar statues gracing each side of the sanctuary, everyday thoughts and images fill my mind providing fleeting relief from the reality of why we are here. I think about it being a typical summer day for Erie. Thunderstorms are predicted for later in the afternoon, well after the funeral will end.

I silently ponder over why the air is always so stale in church even though there are fans churning high overhead. I wonder if my children are reminiscing about their early childhood rites of passage played out within these walls. Does Wayne remember when the nuns were so pleased he played *Stairway to Heaven* at a school event while the young lay teachers sat in the audience remembering hearing this same song at the local hot spot? Luckily, it was an instrumental rendition with no words to reveal the meaning of the song. Does Ed remember trying to lower the flag on a windy day when all of a sudden he became airborne? Does Le'Anne remember her first day of kindergarten? Do they remember Melanie's first communion? I remember it all.

The priest is not someone we know from our past connection to the church. He asked what he could say about our daughter, Melanie. I told him we have a eulogy; we will say the words to honor her life. He sadly reveals he does more funerals then baptisms nowadays, revealing the signs of an aging neighborhood.

I turn around in the pew and notice the extended families of my previous two husbands. I spot friends from work, as well as friends who are on the same spiritual path. I also notice a few people I can't place. The combined spiritual presence of all these people creates a spiritual bond of love and support that I can feel, and desperately need at this time. I realize that the church acts as a broker to provide group support for our spiritual needs. Fortunately, any leftover negative feelings from my former two husbands have been expunged and oblation obtained. We gather here in peace to celebrate the short 23 years of Melanie's life.

As the people enter the church, an inspirational song is playing in the background. Everything seems surreal, unconnected. This is just a dream, right? I'll wake up and everything will be as before. But, I am awake and it's not a dream.

The Eulogy

Melanie's Uncle Jim reads the words written for this moment. He starts by saying, "These words are expressed by Melanie's mother.

Within the last month, Melanie decided to get a tattoo consisting of two dolphins riding the top of a wave. She was quite delighted as it was the first thing she showed us upon our return from France.

Hanging on the wall of my office is the Wildlife of the World calendar. To my amazement, the animal depicting July is the dolphin. In Native American lore, dolphin stands for manna, life force. We learn there is no limit to our reality. By changing the rhythm of our breath we can enter into other realities. Grandmother Moon gave Dolphin the job of being our link with the Creator.

Melanie came into this world during a full moon phase and chose to leave during another full moon phase. Perhaps Melanie has a special relationship with Grandmother Moon too. Perhaps she learned a new rhythm and opened to the light to enter a new and different place from the one she has known. Perhaps the dolphin is an affirmation of the new job our Creator has given Melanie.

May we all have the faith to KNOW within our hearts…that our beloved Melanie…has transcended the bounds and limitations of the human body to discover a new and different life free of the restrictions from whence she came. It is my belief that Melanie has chosen the role of being OUR link, that she will always be with us to guide us along our journey in becoming one with the Creator.

Because she was in the hospital, Melanie missed one of her major life passages, her high school graduation. It was difficult for her not to be present in person to receive this diploma of completion, difficult not being able to share the joy with her friends. Her latest life passage was to leave the Earth Plane. However difficult it is for us, we must accept her decision. May we feel her guiding us on our way. May she continue to feel our love. May this farewell ceremony stand as a tribute not only to her old life, but to her new one as well. May we all learn the rhythm and be open to the light of the Creator. I know God blesses our beloved Melanie. She will live in our hearts forever."

Although it appeared Jim was having a hard time speaking, he continued by saying, "These words are expressed by her Aunt Karen: In a perfect world, there would be no weeping because none of our loved ones would ever have to leave us. There would be no more pain. There would be no such disease as Ataxia trying to limit the voices of my beautiful nieces.

Everyday there would be sunshine and happiness, but even a little rain can give us a beautiful rainbow. Sometimes life's disappointments and tragedies can make our lives richer and more complete, no matter how hard they are to comprehend.

A perfect world would be boring and everyone knows how much Melanie hated to be bored. Melanie can look down on us now and be with whomever she wants, whenever she wants, and she never has to be bored again. She will be way too busy keeping track of us while she has found the ultimate perfect world."

o o o o o

Never in all those years of attending church and its numerous school events did I ever envision returning so soon to bury my youngest child. It's astounding how life plays out with its roller coaster twists-and-turns and its high-highs and low-lows. Not only does it take my breath away and jerks me to and fro, it also tests my spiritual beliefs to my vibral core...my very soul.

Journal Entry–July 10, 2004

Two days after Melanie's burial. I sit here with the copies of the death certificate in my hand. They read, "Melanie Jean Rosthauser died July 2, 2004." How does one begin–at the end with death? Or the beginning with birth? Or are both the same? The end of one way and the beginning of another.

Our Loved Ones

We cry with joy when they arrive. Why do we cry with sorrow when they leave? Do we cry for them...or us? We only feel our sorrow. We do not truly know what goes on in the hearts of others. We may fool ourselves into believing we can read the signs. If so, I need new glasses...bigger bifocals.

Intuition

It is said that it's the most difficult to help those closest to you because you are too emotionally involved. Grandmother Twylah Nitsch couldn't help her son. I couldn't help my daughter. What benefit is it to help others with their pain and suffering if you cannot help your own? Melanie would not confide in me. She refused to open up as to what was going on inside. The stab wound–even IT refused to open up. Instead, she died of massive internal bleeding. Till the end; no, even in the end, she kept it all inside.

A small amount of blood was shed on the outside. A minute indication of what was taking place on the inside. This is the way she chose to live her life–and to end her life.

How did I get to this moment? The Sages say we plan our life before we arrive on this Earth Plane. If so, why would I choose such a difficult one laden with numerous pain-filled challenges beginning with my childhood?

Chapter 2

My parents met while working at American Bridge Company during World War II. My father was too old to go to war and my mother was a *Rosie-the-Riveter* working on LST's (Landing Ship Tanks) for the war effort. He had already experienced a full life and I believe he must have been in a mid-life crisis at the time of their meeting. Hell, if the truth were known, he must have had raging testosterone his whole life! Skeletons in the closet revealed that he had been married several times (not sure if he ever divorced) and had several children with several women. These lost children eventually searched him out to obtain family medical history or to satisfy their curiosity surrounding their biological father. We never knew when another "sister" would pop-up. The housekeeper even became pregnant by my father. In fact, this "sister" is only nine months older than me!

Dad was deemed a genius by his business partners who attended his funeral. We lovingly referred to him as the "mad scientist." It's true. He was very intelligent. Men, like my father, can't be subjected to the day-to-day minutia of life; their minds are too focused on the "what if" of science. Marriage could work if they marry a strong woman to compensate for what they lack in everyday living skills. Unfortunately, my mother was not strong. Aunt Ethel, Dad's sister, shared her opinion that Mom was a woman child who never matured beyond the mental and emotional age of thirteen. What she needed was a strong man to take care of her, perhaps a father figure, since her father died when she was young. I believe the marriage of my parents was a mismatch from the start. So why did they marry? She was pregnant with me. I was the first of five children to this wife. He was 43, she 21.

Family members said my mother loved being pregnant, as it brought attention her way, something she desperately needed. What she didn't possess, was the physical and emotional stamina needed to raise all these children.

After work, Dad would sequester himself in his lab. For the most part, he was inaccessible as a father. He was the strong silent type. She was the drama queen, always fighting with the neighbors.

Like all little girls, I probably drew attention wherever I went. What I remembered from those first years is mother calling me a "Jezebel." Even though I didn't know what it meant, her tone suggested that I had earned this wicked name. When frustrated with my saucy behavior she would pronounce, "Who do you think you are, the Queen of Sheba?" I didn't even know who the "Queen of Sheba" was, but I liked being compared to a queen!

To my mother, I was the child who ruined her dreams of the future. Throughout my entire childhood all I ever heard was, "If it wasn't for you, I could have married so and so…if it wasn't for you, I could have gone to…if it wasn't for you, I could have been a contender." She blamed me for all of her unwise choices. I was an innocent child who took on this mantle of guilt at an early age. It ate away at my self-esteem, my confidence, and undermined the core of who I was. I failed to develop a foundation of truth for myself; instead, a hole developed in my spirit.

When I think about it, the plain truth is that my parents should never have had children. I used to say that we were wild weeds growing up, but later changed it to wild flowers as all of us came to blossom despite the poor emotional soil and lack of that fertilizer we all need in abundance–LOVE.

Chapter 3

It was the summer of 1960; ninth grade was now completed. Dad's other sister, Aunt Ruth, was now living in Erie and invited me up to visit for a few weeks. The main attraction of this touristy water town is a sand spit that extends into Lake Erie called Presque Isle or as the locals call it, "the peninsula."

For me, it was love at first sight. I had seen lakes before, but never like this one. The expansiveness of not being able to see the other side took my breath away. Lying on the warm sand listening to the waves gently lapping onto the shore lulled me into a blissful alpha state. It felt like home. Not the house I live in, but HOME.

All too soon, it was time to return to the noise and daily chaos that was generated by my younger siblings. I hesitantly approached my aunt and asked if I could live in Erie, as I couldn't bear the thought of not being close to this magnificent inland sea. A week after starting tenth grade, her response came. Gaining my uncle's permission and my grandfather's agreement to pay for my upkeep, I happily moved to Erie with the thought of never returning.

However, the Fates had something else in store. It was now the summer after tenth grade and I was spending a weekend with my family back home. My cousins were to pick me up on Sunday, but it never happened. Once again, I was stuck in this hellhole; nothing had changed...except me. I was not wanted in Erie, not really wanted at home, as I would just be another mouth to feed. I was just not wanted! It took twenty years to work up the courage to question why I was sent back home. Was I too bad, too much to handle, why...why...why? A gentle smile passed across Aunt Ruth's face as she replied, "You don't know? It was nothing like that. Your father and uncle got into an argument over who was going to claim you on their income tax return. Your father won, so you were sent home." Therefore, I was deemed a business transaction, nothing more.

After graduating from high school in 1963 and spending an enjoyable summer with my friends, it was time to prepare for my first official job starting in September. Where are my fall and winter clothes? They were stored in a large paper bag that sat beside my small doorless bedroom closet. Without these clothes, I had nothing...absolutely nothing...to wear to work. Mom finally confessed to throwing them out. She thought they were garbage...I... don't...think...so. Hell, the whole house stunk of garbage; my room was the cleanest in the house! Then, other things would suddenly disappear like my jewelry, make-up, etc. Coming home from work, I would find my perfume emptied, bath powder sprinkled all over the dresser, personal items disturbed or broken. She blamed my brother. Imagine, with three younger sisters, she placed the blame on my brother, a young boy who would have no interest in such things!

The assassination of President Kennedy changed the nation and it was a year of change for me also. My boyfriend was drafted into the Vietnam War and I wasn't happy in my job. And as always, Mom was on my case. If I would chose a neighbor's house for my date to pick me up in peace, my mother would lay in wait, yelling out the door so my date could hear, "What's the matter? Are you ashamed of us? Aren't we good enough for your date? Remember, men only want one thing!" Yes, I was ashamed. Not because we were poor or garnered hand-me-down furniture and received food baskets during the holidays, but I was ashamed of the way *she* behaved. I knew if I were ever to get married, I would have to get out of that house.

And get out is what I did! With trepidation, once again I turned to Aunt Ruth and asked, "If I paid room and board, could I return to Erie?" The answer was yes. This time, control was in my hands. I was paying my way. No handouts.

Within two weeks of moving, I had a job and things were going just fine. Then, uh oh...there it is again...that nagging inner voice proclaiming, "Jean, you are not happy in what you are doing, what are you going to do about it?" What am I going to do about it indeed? I wished to share an apartment with a female co-worker, but felt I wasn't making enough money to fully support myself...pay rent, utilities, food, etc. Therefore, I took the easy way out... only it wasn't.

I met my husband at work. He was in engineering, I worked in accounting. After a year, we were married, three months short of my twentieth birthday.

On the day of the dress rehearsal, I sat on the front porch and wondered how to get out of this marriage. I *knew* it was not the right thing to do. He was already beating me. My family turned their heads on the matter, which made me think I deserved it, that the fault lies with me. After running through the list of people who came from out-of-town, caterers to be cancelled, the amount of money already expended, and the receipt of a special blessing from the Pope, I knew the blame would be placed on me, not on the one who beat me. Uneasy about my future, I proceeded with the wedding.

Two children and ten years later, I finally worked up the courage to leave. A lack of self-worth kept me bonded to him, along with that mantle of infantile guilt that followed me into adulthood and led me to believe that somehow it was my fault he beat me. When our children started showing symptoms relating to the dysfunctional relationship, I knew things couldn't get any worse. Somehow, we would leave. No Papal blessing could save this marriage!

I went from hobnobbing with local politicians to pulling a red wagon to the laundry mat, as I no longer had a car. We received no monetary support, but somehow the boys and I managed. At the time Ed was eight and Wayne was four. With the responsibility of raising the boys alone, traveling to the other end of town on a bus to work, and ending the day with tucking the boys into bed, I was left feeling emotionally and physically depleted. I felt all alone. Hell, we had no emotional or family support; we *were* alone! Even my dreams reflected these feelings of helplessness. I had a reoccurring dream about the boys and I being on a beach when a tidal wave suddenly appears on the horizon. We needed to be safe, protected so we ran toward the lighthouse steps. I always woke-up at this point so I never knew if we made it or not.

The hole in my spirit grew larger, leaving an emptiness that begged to be filled. I felt overwhelmed and didn't know where to turn. Organized religion didn't fill my void. I was baptized Episcopalian as an infant; I was baptized Baptist in my early teens, a baptized Presbyterian in my late teens, and converted to Catholicism for this marriage. Somehow, all these initiations into organized religion couldn't stop the hole from widening or soothe my aching soul. What I didn't understand is that I lacked a solid foundation and it was up to me to build it...but how?

Chapter 4

About a year after the divorce, I started dating a man eight years younger than myself. Although, he too was an engineer, he was the exact opposite of my first husband. This man did not drink, did not smoke, did not carouse, and had control of his money. After several months of dating, we planned to marry the following fall. This was his first marriage and he wanted children right away, so I sought advice from my doctor as I had been on the pill for many years. The doctor's reply was that I might not start my period again or I may have trouble conceiving so *we* decided to go off the pill. Those Fates really must have had it in for me, because I had one period and then became pregnant. I morally wouldn't choose an abortion and I couldn't see how I could raise another child on my own. I had recently lost my job and was living on 38 dollars-a-week in unemployment compensation.

This happened around the same time I began growing tired of his extreme attachment to his family and was thinking of perhaps ending our relationship. It was extremely difficult to tell his family about our situation because he never told them of our planned marriage. At the time, I didn't interact with them much because they thought he was being taken advantage of by a divorced woman with two children. They thought he didn't have enough life experience to recognize this and they were trying to protect him. On the night before the wedding, his father proclaimed, "My son is making the biggest mistake of his life." My father-in-law didn't talk to me until six months after the wedding.

It's funny, my first husband separated me from my family and this husband tried to separate me from my friends. Our social life revolved around his family, we didn't visit with friends anymore. However, I did manage to have a small circle of women from work with whom I shared common interests.

This husband was a good father to the children when they were young, but had trouble relating to them as they grew into their middle teens. He is passive-aggressive and a man-child. Isn't it interesting that I could see this at the end of the marriage instead of at the beginning? I have since learned to stop projecting what I want in a person and see what is truly there.

Several years into our marriage that old nagging feeling raised its head again. I was now a mother of four, in a satisfying job, but still feeling incomplete. Although being a mother and wife were pleasant, it wasn't the end all for me. There must be more to life than this.

I started searching for something to satisfy that hole within, that hole that yelled out to be filled. I wanted to understand the reason for my first marriage. Why did I have to go through all that physical and mental turmoil? Why, in the midst of this second marriage filled with wonderful children, a nice house, and a rewarding job, did I still feel incomplete?

The local spiritual bookstore became a starting point for my search. I attended various workshops to develop my inner knowing, bought books on spirituality, and learned how to meditate. I attended lectures by various guest speakers. One speaker, in particular, brought a nugget of truth to my attention.

Chapter 5

The bookstore was having a quest speaker, AmyLee (Oma Lee). After her presentation, you could schedule a reading if so desired. I desired. AmyLee is of Mohawk descent and the last in her family's lineage of woman who dedicate their lives to taking care of the Earth and all that's on it.

Her reading turned out to be quite different from ones I have had before. As Spirit "spoke," AmyLee burned various symbols onto a spirit shield. The shield consists of a wooden twig bent into a circle. Inside the circle is a piece of leather attached to the wood by sinew. When Spirit was finished, AmyLee began to explain what each symbol meant.

My shield is unusual in that it displays a woman whose face is half-hidden by a blanket. AmyLee explained that I am not revealing my true self. This image combined with the other symbols seemed to perplex her. She stated she would be coming by this way again in three months and would like to do another reading for me.

Time passed quickly; AmyLee was back in town for a few days. Off I went with shield in hand, eager to hear what she had to say. This time it was quite different! The image she etched on the other side of my shield was that of a full-faced woman holding up her hand. It showed vibrations emitting from the hand. She stated, "Jean, you have the gift of healing, but you are hiding who you really are." Perhaps I am. I am so busy trying to be who everyone wants me to be that I don't know who I truly am...so I began the quest to find out.

The third weekend of April 1991 had me driving to Hawk Hollow near Tippecanoe–a very small dot on the map in southeastern Ohio. AmyLee was conducting a weekend retreat on meeting our animal spirit guide. She is about my age, has a naturally soothing voice, and has gentle eyes and long brown hair that hangs below her waist. She takes in wounded birds of prey and nurtures them back to health before releasing them on their way. I wondered if this is what she did with her workshop participants also.

During the two-day event, she helped us hone our spiritual awareness by passing around a basket of small quartz crystals. We were to choose one and hold it in our hand until we felt we were one with it. Then all the crystals went back into the basket. Once again, the basket went around so we could retrieve *our* crystal. To my amazement, I had no problem finding my friend again.

As the weekend wound down, the ten women in attendance were asked to pick a blank medicine shield from the pile that sat outside AmyLee's office. Each woman waited her turn to carry her chosen shield into AmyLee to have their particular spirit guide burned into the leather.

Finally, it was my turn. I handed over the shield to AmyLee. She studied it a few seconds and then started to burn an image of a wolf. As we focused on the image materializing on the leather, she remarked, "Look at this, the leather is also in the shape of a wolf. You have two wolves as your spirit guide, one male and one female...balanced energy." I mentioned that I had a reoccurring dream of walking along a path of dark fertile soil in a dappled shaded forest consisting of tall trees supporting a canopy of cooling leaves. In this dream, there is always a wolf standing on the path in front of me, turning his head to look back to see if I am following and a wolf standing behind me, prodding me to move forward on the path. AmyLee asked if I had ever heard of a woman named Twylah Nitsch? She suggested I might want to look her up as I live on Seneca Land...Erie, PA. In earlier times, the people who occupied this southern strip of land bordering Lake Erie were called the Eriez Indians...the Cat People...the Seneca. I thanked AmyLee for the weekend and couldn't wait to tell my friend Susan about the experience.

As it turned out, the same weekend I was encamped with AmyLee, several of my friends, including Susan, attended the first Wolf Song–a Peace Elders Council. Elders from around the world gathered on the Cattaraugus Indian Reservation in western New York to further the goal of peace and unity. Several of the Elders who attended Wolf Song also spoke before the United Nations on this topic.

My friends returned from this event talking incessantly about the originator, a woman named Twylah Hurd Nitsch, as the gathering took place on her land. Twylah is a Native American of Seneca descent and Clan

Mother of the Seneca Wolf Clan. Instruction in the Wolf Clan Lodge centers on Earth Medicine.

In consulting with my friend, Susan, on the meaning of Earth Medicine, we concluded that we were never actually given a formal definition other then self-survival. We were to experience for ourselves what this term meant. Native American culture regards all of nature as their teacher. Examples of this include the Creature Teachers, Tree People, and Rock People. For instance, by watching our Creature Teacher, Spider, weave her web, women have learned how to weave baskets. Likewise, the Tree People guided the Native Americans in the development of their personal growth. The mighty oak tree stands tall and strong while the willow knows how to bend. These traits are also needed in life. Year after year, ring after ring, the trees were a constant reminder of how we grow.

As I listened to my friends' stories of their weekend, I became captivated with what they had learned. I couldn't help but wonder, what kind of name is Twylah Hurd Nitsch? It just didn't sound Indian to me. What kind of name is this for a Medicine Woman? Is she truly a native Medicine Woman, I wondered? As they talked about what had taken place, I listened with fascination and thought it would be interesting to meet this woman one day. After all, AmyLee said I should look her up.

o o o o o

It was a sweltering hot day in late summer. The kind of day that makes you wish you had a swimming pool, the kind of day that if you are too active you will surely have to change your sweat-drenched shirt numerous times. In other words, the kind of day that you should just stay put. Did I do this? Nooo.

On this blistering Sunday, my friend Laurie called and asked if I wanted to attend a Pow Wow being held on the Cattaraugus Indian Reservation. A Pow Wow is the Native American way of getting together, dancing, singing, renewing old friendships, and making new ones. Pow Wow singers, drummers, and dancers take center stage during this event. It's one hell of a festival!

Even though I didn't want to venture out of my cool comfortable home, I accepted her invitation because I thought we might run into Twylah Nitsch. After an hour into our air-conditioned northeastward journey along I-90, I mentioned to Laurie and her young son, Jack, that perhaps Twylah would attend. Laurie doubted this as Twylah had recently broken her kneecap from a fall down the stairs. We talked a bit about the mishap as I clung to my hope of meeting her.

Upon arriving, we parked the car in the designated field, paid our entrance fee, and proceeded to browse the many booths displaying handmade jewelry, feather headdresses, pipes, herbs, and other native items of interest. After taking in all the items in all the booths, I returned to the first booth and purchased a necklace made out of bone with a bear claw hanging from the center. The necklace served as a reminder that I had the capacity to quiet my mind, enter the silence, and *know*. Jack had a hard time deciding on his purchase, but finally settled on an arrowhead.

Our growling stomachs indicated it was time to enjoy the great food served at these events. We sampled the buffalo burgers and Indian tacos. We finished with fried bread and ghost bread. They are the same, except ghost bread has powdered sugar sprinkled on top. Soon the drums began beating, indicating that it's time for the dance contests to start.

As we tromped through the crisp, sunburned grass to reach the temporary grandstand, our shoes left a lingering trail of fine dust. Although the hot sun high in the sky blinded our eyes, we couldn't help but notice a blue tarp crudely erected to provide shade to a small section of seats. For whom, I wondered? As we neared the bleachers, Laurie let out a gasp of delight, for sitting in the blue shade was Grandmother Twylah (Twy) surrounded by her entourage of protégés. Grandmother or Gram is a term of endearment showing respect for an Elder. I damn well made sure we sat as near to Grandmother Twylah as possible without invading her space.

Soon the drums began to beat louder, the singers joined in with their high-pitched chants as the Grand Entry of the dancers began. All the attending nations (they are not called tribes as the word tribe pertains to Africa) paraded around the field to display their handmade costumes created for each particular dance. Dances are either for men or for women. There was judging and a winner chosen for each round. My favorite women dances are the Jingle Dance, Fancy Shawl Dance, and the Northern Traditional Dance.

The dress for the Jingle Dance features rows of jingle cones. The cones may have originally been the metal lids of Copenhagen snuff, but are now made of other metals. They also contain decorations of ribbon, appliqué, and beadwork and can have matching leggings, moccasins, purses, and hair ornaments. Feathers adorn the headdresses and are made into fans, which are held high during the honor beats of the song. The unique jangle of the cones makes this a fascinating round.

The dress for the Fancy Shawl Dance consists of an elaborately beaded dress and beaded moccasins complemented by beautifully embroidered or decorated long fringed shawls. The shawl represents the Spanish influence of the Southwest. These colorful outfits compliment the spirited twirling and prancing of this fast-paced dance.

The stately Northern Traditional Dance involves a slow-moving bouncing step, rhythmically dipping and swaying to the beat of the drum. Traditional dresses are made out of buckskin and are heavily decorated with beading, quillwork, bone, or shells. The colors for this dance tend to be more subdued than in the other dances.

I became so entranced with all the pageantry, I almost forgot my purpose for attending...to meet Twylah Hurd Nitsch. As the event progressed, the opportunity came. One of the protégés recognized Laurie and came over to say hello. Grandmother Twylah followed. We struck up a conversation. I found a lot of vitality packed into her short slight stature. Her long silver hair was twisted into a bun and held in place on the side of her head by a large silver barrette. Her face carried heavy deep wrinkles that seemed to hold the wisdom of the ages, but by far her most impressive feature was her deep dark brown penetrating eyes. How they sparkled with vim and vigor! However, one should not be fooled, as they could reach deep into your soul to determine your Truth. On her finger sat a large silver ring consisting of two long slender turquoise stones. She was friendly, charming, and filled with so much positive energy that it overflowed to everyone nearby. As she placed my right hand between her two hands she proclaimed, "It's a pleasure to meet you," and seemed in no hurry to let go.

We talked for a few minutes and as we were saying our farewells. Twylah invited us to her home to see a map of the United States that was gifted to her by a friend. It depicts the coming changes that will take place along our coasts within our lifetime. What an unexpected invitation! I just met her and she invited us to her house! Upon arrival at her modest white clapboard home, we were met by her *protectors*. They were the inner-circle people who tried to chase away the uninvited wayward seekers who constantly showed up on her doorstep.

While they were trying to shoo us away, Grandmother Twylah intervened. She led us to the map and talked about what it represented. I never give much credence to such predictions as the map displayed, but I listened intently with great respect. I wondered what would cause such a drastic change in our coastlines. We didn't want to overstay our welcome, so we bid good-bye and accepted an invitation to return the following week for evening ceremony.

After being home for a few days, I made a surprising discovery. For a long time, a big old wart had taken-up residence on the tip of the middle finger of my right hand. It had been there for so long I was no longer consciously aware of it. As I glanced down at that finger, the wart had disappeared. There was no sign that it ever existed. No scar...no scab...nothing. Perhaps Grandmother Twylah truly is a Medicine Woman. Perhaps I no longer needed to give the finger to the world!

The Fates that led me to sit out in the middle of that fallow cornfield in the hot midday sun have changed my life forever!

Chapter 6

One invitation to evening ceremony turned into years of traveling back and forth to Twylah's home. I was intrigued by her wisdom and the Native American culture.

The way Twylah came into this world is quite a story—a story she related to me and to the numerous people who came to visit. A man named Running Deer was walking along one day when he stubbed his toe on a rock. He picked up the rock and took it home with him.

The next morning Running Deer took the rock to his neighbor, Moses Shongo, the last recognized Medicine Man of the Seneca Nation. The rock spoke to Moses telling him his daughter was to have a girl. It foretold that the child will be a great teacher and the wisdom she requires is contained within the stone.

Just as the stone predicted, Moses' daughter began labor on her birthday. A baby girl was born to a Native American mother and a Scottish/Oneida father on December 6, 1912. She was named Twylah and given the medicine name of Yehwehnode, *She Whose Voice Rides on the Wind*. It would be her destiny to grow into this name.

When Twylah was three, she came down with whooping cough and started choking. Her grandfather saved her life with mouth-to-mouth resuscitation. He then prophesied to his family that her breath is now his breath and that she will carry on the teachings. People will come from all over the world to hear her words. Her life will contain many hard lessons; she will go deaf, she will be blind, she will be crippled, but she will recover from them all. These lessons will help her to have empathy and understanding of those who seek her out.

Twylah's grandparents taught her Earth Medicine, the intuitive interconnection with all things. With eyes to see, ears to hear, and hearts to listen, Nature shows us the way. The Creator/Great Mystery is not outside us…up there beyond reach…but within ourselves. She learned to experience knowledge for herself and to take the time to listen. Listen to the Earth, listen to the trees, flowers, birds, and all the creature teachers that are calling out to us, just waiting to impart the wisdom they have learned through the ages. The rocks and stones also call, for they too are of the Creator.

Twylah learned she could find her own solutions to the questions life presented her. Her grandparents taught her that the most important thing to recognize was her own Truth, that voice within. Twylah learned what her Truth was—that she was gifted with wisdom, integrity, stability, and dignity.

Twylah went on to relate how she was disciplined when she was little. It seems she was always getting into things, but she was not spanked…ever. Instead, she would be asked, "Are you happy in what you are doing?" If she said "yes" they would say, "Maybe you should think again. Maybe you don't understand how you might get hurt." So Twylah was warned that if she continued, she would be responsible for the consequences that would follow. That is how she learned the difference between right and wrong. Right is comfort…wrong is pain.

When Twylah was five-years-old, the government took her away from the reservation to attend school. Isn't it hard to believe that well into the 20th century the government was still trying to make the "red folk" white? She was placed into the home of a white family in Buffalo, NY. This was her first experience with different cultures. Living in the homes of white people during the school year was a dramatic culture shock to her. She learned that not all people live alike nor do they all think alike.

The first family Twy lived with had a daughter her age. The girl was always being spanked by her mother. Twylah couldn't understand why there was always so much yelling and screaming going on in that house. It seemed to Twylah that the mother lacked an inner truth she could follow and depend upon.

Twylah said she learned about competition and jealousy from living in that house. The little girl was forced to share her bed with Twylah. Twy realized that she was in *her space*. The girl's parents forced her to take piano lessons which she hated. Twy would listen to the girl practice and then taught herself how to play. One day, the parents asked both of them to perform for some guests. Because the little girl hated the piano, she played badly, and because Twy loved it, she played from her heart. After that day, the girl never liked her.

Gram realized there would never be any possibility of friendship between them because there was no *wholeness* in the girl's culture. Everyone was in competition with each other, rather than in *cooperation,* as Gram had been taught.

Gram also discovered she was quite different from the other children at school. She didn't talk like them, didn't gossip, and didn't giggle. She never said anything unless she was spoken to first. She already possessed the wisdom to discern that some teachers were only interested in getting their paychecks.

Every summer she would return to the reservation and hear the lessons of her Elders. She recognized that many people talked about how much they loved their children, but few understood love. She thought that society is bent on destroying the self-esteem within their children; that children are deprived of the love and comfort they need. They're told they don't know anything, they're stupid, and so they begin to think they're unworthy of being treated with respect. This kind of treatment can make children doubt their own Truth. Gram said that all children are born knowing what their Truth is, but it can be compromised when people are constantly lying to them.

Twylah was twelve-years-old when her Grandfather dropped his robe (died). She was away at school. Before he passed, he reminded her of her destiny. He said it was time to start writing down the teachings, so they wouldn't become lost. Native American teachings were traditionally passed down orally, there was no written history. She vaguely recalls making a promise that she would. Little did she know what her future would bring!

In the ensuing years, Twylah became very busy living in the white man's world. While in high school, she lost her hearing for eight months due to complications from mumps. Since Twy couldn't hear in the physical, she began to write poetry. Twylah began to listen to her inner voice, her Spirit Teachers, and was able to *hear* them more clearly. They spoke to her in rhyme.

Later, she became blind. I believe it was due to a flash bulb going off too close to her face. She doesn't remember how long the blindness lasted because she said time loses meaning when you can't see the clock. Blindness taught her that you have to *see,* not just look. When blind, all of your other senses are magnified, thus increasing your sensitivity to the beauty and perfection of the world.

Twylah went on to marry a man of Dutch descent. However, his mother disowned him because he had married an *Indian*. After Twy's last child was born, she became crippled. The doctor had given her a spinal block for the delivery and it caused an injury. She didn't walk for three years. She felt that it was her destiny to teach people how to heal themselves of multiple disabilities and that she needed to experience some of those disabilities herself. The lesson she learned was to become more aware, more sensitive, and more compassionate towards others. She maintains that every time she lost something, she never asked, "Why is this happening to me?" Instead, she thought, "What can I learn from this?" After all, her grandfather had said she would overcome all these handicaps, so she trusted that she would. And she did!

Twylah was raised in both the religion of her people and in Christianity. She thought Jesus Christ was a good man who got a lousy deal. The main drawback she saw in Christianity was that the image was of a male. In her culture, the Supreme Being contains both male and female energy. She often said that the worst thing that happens to humankind is when the truth within is taken away and put out on a cloud. People who are looking for God look in the wrong places, because God is and always was and forever will be... within. Separation rather than unity, control rather than freedom, became the way the word of God was spread.

Gram went on to say that western cultures want to divide everything into light and dark...good and evil...the right way and the wrong way. They do not realize that everything is light; we are beings of light. Gram believed we have no darkness within us, that we have lessons and challenges within us. We make the decision to overcome our challenges, our fears, or to remain the same.

While raising her children and working as a recreation supervisor living in white society with her husband, Twy had forgotten the teachings. She had decided she didn't want her voice to be heard in the world. She felt that nobody was really listening anyway. It seemed to her that most people thought they already knew everything and that their eyes and ears were closed to the Truth. She began to feel that what she had to say wasn't important. She struggled with her predicted destiny; she needed to be writing, but she

21

didn't want to write. Then a chain of events took place and she was no longer able to ignore what was to be. An old friend that she hadn't seen for a long time came to visit. They hugged each other so hard that that he broke two of her ribs. A week later, she fell and injured her kneecap. It was at this point that her destiny spoke out, saying, "You have not been responsible, you have not been disciplined, you must now sit down and do nothing but write." Her limited movement forced her to stay in the house so she began to write down the teachings. She didn't care anymore whether it sounded good or was acceptable to people; she wrote because it was her responsibility to do so.

Twylah didn't like being called a Healer, a Medicine Woman. She thought these words were not an accurate description of what she did. She taught people to give thanks for what they already have. To give thanks is to ask nothing for ourselves, because everything we need is already available from Mother Earth.

Healing means gratitude–gratitude for being allowed to perform this Earthwalk, to be given the gifts of Mother Earth, to know we're walking *with* the Earth, not *on* Her. Gram had said many times that healing is being grateful for being allowed to survive. The clue to survival is in one's own nature, the key to healing is gratitude, the source of which is love within, truth within, and month one was born. Since I was born in the month of November, I came into this world to hear the Truth within and then share it with others. It also means I have magnetism to attract and release what I need/don't need and I must learn to listen within to discern my personal rhythm and timing to know when I am to share my knowledge with others. The *Pathway of Peace* wheel helps us to discover our mission in life, our Earth Path, based on our birth colors.

All of the intuitive exercises done in an *Intensive* were developed by Gramto bring to light our personal internal truths. The teachings are placed on a medicine wheel, a circle containing twelve spokes. The circle represents wholeness, completion. The middle of the wheel represents the vibral core, the center of our being. Medicine means anything that improves one's connection to all of life involving the mind, body, and spirit. It helps to bring about personal strength and understanding to our existence. During this "brain fry" a person tries to obtain knowledge about who am I, from where did I come, why I am here, and what does the future have in store for me? You know…those familiar philosophical questions we all ask ourselves at some point in life.

Chapter 7

I was greatly attracted to Twylah and her land. Late summer found me driving up to her place with a friend or two in tow to attend evening ceremony. It seemed that the focus of our conversation during the drive would become the topic of Twylah's lesson that night. It never failed. For instance, if we saw crows on the way up, we would discuss their number and direction in which they were flying to figure out the message for us. I'm not sure we ever did, but upon arrival at Twy's, lo-and-behold her topic for the evening would center on the meaning of Crow. After one of her students conducted evening ceremony, Gram would say, "Let's talk about crow tonight. Does anyone know what crow stands for?" Laurie piped up, "We were just discussing crow on our way up here. I think it stands for Earth Law-sacred law." Earth Law is where we come from and sacred law is listening to the voice within. The two must be in harmony with each other. Then off we would go…losing track of time discussing crow medicine.

Soon summer was over and the leaves were revealing their true colors as Mother Nature prepared to hibernate for another cycle of seasons. During this transition, I felt a need for some one-on-one, so I registered for an *Intensive Weekend* at Twylah's, otherwise known as a "brain fry."

An *Intensive* teaches us we are part of the whole. The circle symbolizes the idea of the whole. The lessons are inspired by the ancient Seneca Indian philosophy of respect for all life. We learn to understand the harmonious interdependence amongst all creation. The total process of life's sustenance comes from the same source. It emits from every manifestation, seen or unseen, felt or unfelt, as a life energy. Things that appear inert to the average onlooker are endowed with the same life essence (rocks, soil, air, etc.). It is every person's goal to become a whole being.

The foundation of Gram's teachings is found in her *Cycles of Truth* and *Pathway of Peace Lessons*. The *Cycles of Truth* medicine wheel is based on the month one was born. Since I was born in the month of November, I came into this world to hear the Truth within and then share it with others. It also means I have magnetism to attract and release what I need/don't need and I must learn to listen within to discern my personal rhythm and timing to know when I am to share my knowledge with others. The *Pathway of Peace* wheel helps us to discover our mission in life, our Earth Path, based on our birth colors.

All of the intuitive exercises done in an *Intensive* were developed by Gram to bring to light our personal internal truths. The teachings are placed on a medicine wheel, a circle containing twelve spokes. The circle represents wholeness, completion. The middle of the wheel represents the vibral core, the center of our being. Medicine means anything that improves one's connection to all of life involving the mind, body, and spirit. It helps to bring about personal strength and understanding to our existence. During this "brain fry" a person tries to obtain knowledge about himself/herself such as: Who am I? Where did I come? Why I am here? What does the future have in store for me? You know…those familiar philosophical questions we all ask ourselves at some point in life.

Gram's students are dedicated to share what they learn. We were told to go out and express the teachings in our lives. She often told us, "What good is knowledge if it is not shared?"

So here I was, on a cold November evening, driving up to the reservation after work. During this silent twilight expedition, I felt suspended in time. This had happened on other trips to the reservation. For some reason this stretch of I-90 in New York always felt like the Twilight Zone…or should I say the Twylah Zone! The trip seemed to take forever or else I would suddenly find myself pulling up to the tollbooth at the state line and wondered how I got there so fast. While in this time warp, I mused over my purpose for the *Intensive*. What did I want to accomplish from the weekend? What was I searching for? What niche inside me sought fulfillment? Or is it that I was just curious, open to other possibilities? I just didn't know…but I was confident that I would receive some answers.

Her private driveway passed by the side of the house and led me through the golden beacon of light shining out from the large plate glass living room window. I hurriedly parked the car and unloaded my gear in near total darkness. This was the country. There were no streetlights dimly lighting the way. I sought my way to the light shining from the side door of this safe haven, eager to begin.

Gram greeted me at the door with her smiling eyes. "Well, here she is," she said. "I just about gave up on you. Come in and meet the other women." Two are counselors from New Jersey and the third, a counselor from New York. I wondered how I will fit into this group of professional counselors. I wanted to major in psychology in college but dropped out. Gram says there are no coincidences…everything happens for a reason. I dumped my overnighter and blankets on the floor of Twylah's flamingo pink living room. The upstairs bedrooms were already taken so I camped out on the living room couch.

The others had already received their "colors." It was Gram's bedtime, so she asked a helper to bring me up to where the others had ended for the day. The women asked if they could sit in and observe as the more times you hear a teaching, the better you understand.

I completed the medicine wheel chart based on thirteen colors and the meanings assigned to each that revealed my seven personal gifts of birth, my five latent talents, and a boundary skill appropriate for my mission/lessons in life. The boundary color helps to identify the direction for personal growth, how much we let in or out before we say "no more." Unfortunately, I have a difficult boundary color…crystal. This means I must see the total picture, have total clarity before I make a decision. As I reflect back on my life, I can discern this to be true. I stay way too long in a situation, making sure it is no longer "growing corn" before making the decision to move on. I let people impinge on me too long before saying "no more." After receiving my colors, it was "no more" for tonight. It was time to take in some zzz's.

The dawning light saw us making our way into the kitchen to seek a seat around the white cast iron kitchen table. Gram joined us in light conversation as we ate breakfast and downed our morning coffee. Then she said, "Listen, we have a lot to cover today." So off we went. We didn't need to be told twice. We moved into a small sparse room that contained a table and some chairs. The table was barely large enough for the five of us to gather around as our lesson books were spread out to write. Gram reiterated what we learned the night before. She said, "Your latent talents are your mission in life and are developed during your Earth Path." A woman asked, "When you talk about lessons, just what do you mean?" Gram replied, "Lessons are nothing more than daily experiences based upon Challenge-Change-Choice-Commitment, which are the Four Winds of Growth. These gifts do not change because they produce our stability and focus upon our inner-truth." What in the heck does that mean, I wondered to myself?

Okay, let's work this through. Pink is my eighth color on the wheel, which stands for my first latent talent. This color defines how my learning potential can be developed more fully this lifetime. I learned from the descriptions that pink indicates I am a worker and creator. "Is this true?" I asked Gram. I know I am a worker, but I never thought of myself as a creative person. She replied, "Jean, by developing your creativity you will gain illumination. Your choices will bring about options which will give you insight to discover your Truths. Gaining foresight will present opportunities for expression and sharing." Wow! This is a lot to digest for just one color, right? I can honestly say, that all these years later, I am still gaining insight to understand just what this all means. Remember, this is just *one* of the lessons I am to learn this lifetime and this is just *one* layer of that lesson. As we grow in awareness, the lessons become more profound. Gram then went on to decipher the eighth color for the others.

"Now listen here," she said tapping her finger on the table for emphasis. When we enter this Earthwalk, we know our time of birth, place, parents, weight, sex, health, image, mission, and at what time we return to spirit. I said I felt I didn't belong with my parents; there must have been a mistake at the hospital. "No, Jean. There are no mistakes," she said. "You have the parents you picked out before your birth to present the lessons you needed to grow into adulthood." I was on a roll. I said, "If we choose our image, I have to be more precise the next time. In the past, I must have been born into a time period when it was fashionable to be fat and I was thin. So this time around, I asked to be born fat. What I should have asked was to weigh what is fashionable for the time." Everyone howled. Gram rolled her eyes!

Time became meaningless; we were so engrossed in the teachings that we ran way past lunch. After a break, we reconvened for the next exercise devoted to discovering our animal totems, our personal creature teachers. Gram was taught to honor every living thing as a teacher. Animals form practices in their lives from which we can learn. To look upon a creature teacher for guidance is to assimilate the strength and harmony of that animal.

The Creature Teacher Wheel is made up of fifty-two little circles forming a larger circle. Gram instructed us to number nine circles at random to intuitively select our animal totems. "Now don't take a lot of time doing this, let your intuition be your guide. Don't think about it." Each animal has assigned attributes and where the nine animals sat on our personal wheel had specific meaning for us.

For instance, horse sits in the West on my personal wheel. The West represents our goals. Horse stands for strength, responsibility, and power. Perhaps that's why we still measure the power of an engine in *horsepower*. Ford brought back the Mustang—a muscle car full of horsepower. Through horse, we *learn* to release our burdens, *honor* them as carriers of Truth, *know* their dependability, and *hear* our future. Horses are the transporters of Truth and are depicted as carrying Shamans to heaven.

The lesson on Horse reminds me of a meditation I engaged in at AmyLee's. I had a vision of being pulled in a cart by a team of three brown horses running at a fast pace when they suddenly then took off for the heavens. Through Gram's teaching, I can interpret this vision as my inner knowing (represented by the color brown) leading me to understand (three is the number of change) that I am an instrument of the Great Spirit/the Creator (represented by the skies).

After placing our animal totems on the medicine wheel, we then created an Animal Chart based on each of their attributes. The words that were underlined were then transposed onto a sheet of questions that clarify queries such as, "What is my achievement in life?" The whole procedure turned out to be a very intensive exercise, leaving us confused and exhausted. It took up all of Saturday afternoon.

By early evening Gram's voice had given out, as did our concentration. It was just too much information to absorb in one weekend so we stopped for the day, had a delightful dinner with Gram followed by a quiet evening to reflect on what we had discovered about ourselves.

Sunday morning turned out to be a most delightful time. We were all in good spirits as we began the final countdown. Gram said, "Now go outside and walk the grounds until you find a stone that speaks to you. Bring it back and I will read the personal message the stone has for you." What the heck did this mean? Outside we went, each of us turning in a different direction to seek a stone calling our name. I must have picked up a dozen or more stones before finally settling on one, although I don't recall it speaking out. Maybe I was trying too hard. It was an ordinary rock, not a gemstone, or some other type of fancy boulder. There was nothing on Gram's land that was fancy to the physical eye. The radiance it held was to be felt in the heart, not seen by the eye.

Gram placed the petrified piece of earth I handed her on my stone chart and proceeded to draw some intersecting lines. Then she started to talk. "You are a dreamer and a counselor." She went on to explain what that meant. Then she continued with, "You need to honor your wants in life." She explained that crystal is hard to have as a boundary color. "It's also my boundary color," she revealed. "You allow far too much to happen before you say 'no more.' You have to see the whole picture before proceeding. Jean, you must learn to say 'not now.' Saying 'no' shuts things off forever. Saying 'not now' puts it somewhere in the future to be reconsidered. Harmony must come from the sharing of *who* you are—not *what* you are. This will bring about a completion for you." She went on to reveal, "There is something on your truth line you are not using. It has to do with your wisdom. You need to harmonize your thinking and listening to bring what you say and think out into the open. Through your thoughts you will bring about the action."

The rock reading now complete, there was nothing left to do but say good-bye. As I walked to the car, Twylah called out, "Jean, you are a good woman." I smiled at her as I waved good-bye. That was it. The "brain fry" was over...or was it just beginning?

Chapter 8

Journal Entry–June 12, 1992

Yippee, I got my promotion at work! After temporarily working seven months as an Employment Specialist 2, I finally became permanent.

he way this came about was very unusual. I worked for the Pennsylvania Department of Labor; our bureau's main function was to help people obtain employment and job training. My boss, Linda, and I traveled to Harrisburg to do a presentation on our region's version of a Career Resource Center. This was to be a place where people could get additional help for employment; these new services would be in addition to the other services we already offered. They might consist of helping to write resumes, preparing for an interview, researching job training opportunities, schools, and social services. This was a new initiative for the public employment office in Pennsylvania and offered a chance to showcase my weeks of research.

Each of the state regions (consisting of a certain number of counties) was to present their ideas to the bureau's central office big wigs, those with the power to make it happen. Since Erie was number seven out of eleven regions, I had a chance to hear some of the other presentations before giving mine. In my opinion, the others' plans were either quite elaborate or far-fetched. Some wanted to consult employer groups that, at the time, I didn't even know existed! Remember, I was newbie to the workings of a regional office.

As I sat waiting my turn, I noticed the bureau's movers and shakers were sitting in the front of the room, behind the podium. I was puzzled about the odd room arrangement. As we stood at the podium, we were not able to see the expressions on the faces of those who would ultimately decide whether to accept or reject our ideas. Bummer. When it was time for the Erie Region to do our presentation, my knees started shaking so much I could hardly walk to the front of the room to begin my talk. I haven't been this nervous since I was a junior in high school. As president of my school's Future Homemakers of America (FHA), I was to introduce some candidates for a FHA election held at the Hilton Hotel in downtown Pittsburgh. It was my first attempt at public speaking and my knees were knocking so much I was quite sure I would fall flat on my face. Those exact same thoughts were running through my mind now.

For some crazy reason...probably nerves...I started out by explaining that I've been in this temporary position for only a few months, that I had interviewed for it, but the hiring decision had not yet been made. I said that I better do well today because I had a feeling the job offer would rest on how my presentation was accepted. Everyone chuckled. Holy cow, I can't believe I said that! I thought that I might have embarrassed my boss and now I'll never get the job. Bummer.

I went on to say that because I was still fresh out of the local office, I took a slightly different approach from the others; I took the approach of a job seeker. I could hear voices behind me. Whispers of perhaps that is the approach that should be taken. As I went down the list of what I thought the centers should contain, I could hear grunts coming from my rear. No... it wasn't gas, it was gasps of approval!

Afterwards, two men approached to get my opinion on the computers they had ordered for the centers. Imagine, they asked my opinion! Years later, one of these men would become my last supervisor before retirement; my best ally at work.

I wanted this job in the regional office very much. I saw this position as a chance to reach more of the public because I would be working with all the Employment Interviewers who work with the public in the eleven counties that made up our region. I would be helping them to improve their programs and training them on how to obtain better customer satisfaction.

On the trip home from Harrisburg, I could tell Linda was quite pleased with my presentation but we were both tired and weary so we didn't talk much. After five hours, we finally pulled into my driveway. As I opened the door to leave Linda said, "By the way, you got the job!"

So...on a high note, I leave this afternoon to attend the Women's Council at Grandmother Twylah's place. Life can't get much better!

Journal Entry–June 25, 1992

So much took place at the Council that I couldn't write about it till now. It seems when one goes to Twy's, it always takes time to digest what happens. The seed of the lesson planted doesn't take root right away and may not bloom until years later. This is the nature of her teachings. To embrace the lessons and learn our personal truths would dramatically change our lives. That was a gross understatement.

My friends, Susan and Laurie, attended the Women's Council with me. We arrived with just enough light left in the evening sky to pitch our tent, lay out our sleeping bags, and scope out the outhouse. It had rained earlier in the day and our shoes and socks were so muddy by the time we had finished that we had to leave them outside the tent. When it started to rain again, Laurie advised, "As long as we don't touch the tent material the rain will stay on the outside, we won't get wet."

During the night, I had to use the facility. I picked a spot by the door to sleep for this very reason, as I didn't want to disturb everyone. As I opened the flap and crawled into the rain soaked darkness, I discovered my flashlight didn't produce enough illumination to walk the distance so I decided to do what any red-blooded man would do…only it isn't as easy for a woman!

By midmorning, after tromping through acres of mud, we overheard two women talk about taking a shower. We looked at each other…a shower…we could take a shower? The shower turned out to be a cold water hose hung from a tree. Laurie was not satisfied with this arrangement. She said, "I saw a couple of men walking around the area. There's no shower curtain, I can't do this!" I couldn't stand being caked with mud a second longer and said, "Men or no men, I'm taking a shower." Susan agreed. We could put modesty aside in such dire circumstances. After the cold shower, the sun finally came out and dried up the mud. We soon grew accustomed to walking the distance to the portable outhouses. (Now, I don't want to imply that the Council attendees were all full of it, but by the end of the event *all* the porta-potties were overflowing. Susan said, "It turned out to be a very releasing weekend in more ways than one!")

When registering for this event, we didn't know what to expect. The Council didn't run on a time schedule. Instead, it ran on Indian time. Native Americans do not follow a clock, rather they intuitively sense when the time is right to begin. Several "Grandmothers" spoke. We sat for hours in the teaching lodge on hard backless wooden benches listening to their stories and teachings. When rear ends went numb and our backs could take no more, we would break for a meal and then return to the lodge for more. At night, we learned to dance and sing Indian style. What fun!

Among all the Grandmothers who spoke that weekend, one stood out to me...Grandmother Sara Smith, a Mohawk of the Turtle Clan from Ontario, Canada. Sara stood tall and proud in the middle of the teaching lodge and related that Turtle Clan, like Wolf Clan, cares for the Earth. Grandmother Sara talked about women's role today and ended her presentation with a strawberry ceremony to honor women's Moontime (menses). Sara went on to explain that the June Strawberry Moon illumes a ceremony held to honor the girls who have become women in the past year. The strawberry is a symbol of the Earth with each tiny seed representing one of the Native nations. The color red stands for blood and is the connection to all life energy that flows in and out of our body. The ceremony is also a time for giving and receiving forgiveness. I really can't remember what else she said, only the kind and firm manner in which she said it. After prayers of forgiveness, a bucket of freshly squashed red berries was passed around so each of us could take a scoop full. The cool red juice felt so good going down our parched throats.

Grandmother Sara ended by sharing a give-away gift with us. We were asked to take an envelope out of a basket and then pass it on to the next person. An excited "awe" rose from everyone's lips as they waited their turn at the basket. There must have been a hundred spiritual hungry feminine souls in the lodge that afternoon and Sara had enough envelopes for all of us.

Laurie was the first from our group to pick. "Look, she exclaimed, a butterfly sticker! There have been a lot of butterflies around my house this week. I'll have to look up butterfly to see what message it has for me."

Next was Susan. "I got a twig of cedar," she said softly. "How appropriate, you are our expert plant lady," I replied. Laurie asked, "Do you know what cedar stands for?" Susan replied, "No, but I'm about to find out!"

At last...it was my turn. I closed my eyes, reached in and pulled out an envelope that contained a rough hand cut cloudy green stone. The first thing that came to my mind is that the stone is an emerald, and if this is true, it needs to be returned to Sara. I scheduled a private session with her to discuss the stone and its value.

Sara is a lovely steadfast traditional Elder. She wore a green flower print cotton ribbon dress and sat very erect. She spoke in a soft voice and displayed a large smile. All of her lessons and stories are passed on verbally; we are not allowed to take notes. Sara pointed out that we will remember what we need to remember.

I suggested that she might want the stone back because it may be of monetary value. She looked me in the eye and with a serious tone to her voice said, "I gave this stone to you. You are a healer. The color green represents healing and this stone will assist you in your teachings. I don't know if the stone is an emerald or colored glass, it is yours now."

I felt unworthy to be the keeper of the stone. I didn't want the responsibility it carried. I didn't want to be a healer like Twylah, having strangers in and out of my house all the time. I'm too private a person; I need my quiet time. Besides, my husband would never accept the situation. He doesn't like me having spiritual yearnings; he doesn't like me going to Twy's all the time. It frightens him. Her teachings don't conform to Catholicism.

The stone sat in my dresser drawer for over two years before I pulled it out. I decided to have it set into a ring by a jeweler I trusted. I wanted to honor it in the manner it deserved. It became important to me to find out if the stone truly was an emerald. I went on a mission to find out. Unfortunately, to have it tested would leave marks. I almost gave up. While attending a juried art festival in the fall, I came upon a man who sold gemstones. I held up my hand so he could examine the stone and asked if it was an emerald. He hesitated a bit, looked me in the eyes, and then quietly stated, "Yes, indeed it is an emerald, but I'm sad to inform you that it's an inferior grade B quality." I told him, "I could care less if it were colored glass; it means the world to me." And I meant it.

Chapter 9

Journal Entry–September 26, 1993

A lot has happened since my last entry. I find it so hard to record my thoughts. I told my husband several weeks ago that I wanted a divorce, but he won't listen to my request... he just buries his head in the sand. He is so afraid of dying that he doesn't live. I want the marriage to end quietly...for instance, him accepting a job out of town and we don't follow.

Gram said that to accept and live the teachings would change one's life. We would no longer devote energy to those things that no longer "grow corn." I guess my stagnant marriage fell into that fallow field.

In 1991, my family moved into a bigger house. It was a struggle to get my husband to consent to the move. We had been living in a starter house... three bedrooms, kitchen/dining area, 1 ½ baths, and a living room. As the family expanded, my oldest son, Ed, shifted his bedroom to the basement, Wayne occupied the smallest bedroom and the two girls shared a room. The children were growing bigger and their "toys" were becoming more numerous. I couldn't find a quiet spot to meditate. We had outgrown the house and desperately needed more space.

My husband was hesitant to make the change. He asked, "What if I lose my job, how will we make the payments?" He lamented, "What if I get sick and can't work?" I said don't put those thoughts out into the ethers. Blow them away. In my head, I could hear Gram saying that thoughts are energy and I didn't want to put that kind of energy into action.

He pooh-poohed "my nonsense" as he frowned upon my spiritual quest. He was born and raised Catholic, went to Catholic grade school, Catholic high school, and Catholic college. That's all he knew. He wasn't open to other concepts.

I was raised differently. My parents didn't attend church, although my father did believe in God. As I think back, he lived many of the same principals as Twylah lived; he just didn't put them into words. We kids would attend the closest church, it didn't matter the denomination. I think we attended more for the social then the spiritual, although the spiritual must have rubbed off on us too.

In my first marriage, my husband was Catholic and insisted I convert. Since it didn't matter to me what name my faith carried, I did. What became ironic is that the priest who instructed me in my convert lessons got married before I did. What can I say…it was the sixties!

I was not enamored with the rituals of the Catholic Church. I was used to talking to the Creator, one-on-one. As a young child, I would go out in the woods and sit under three large oak trees whenever I was sad or upset or just needed some of nature's air-conditioning. When my mother yelled at me, I would run away from home to a row of tall dark green pine trees that stood as sentinels along the highway that ran past our property. After being shrouded in their soft aromatic needles for a time, I would slowly make my way back home. It was as if the pines prepared me to endure my mother's wrath. The trees brought peace to my tiny troubled heart.

Now, I have to go through a priest (a mortal) to confess my sins and receive penance. This only made my heart more troubled; it didn't bring peace. I stayed the course for the sake of my children. I wanted them to have a religious foundation; when they grew older they could decide for themselves.

I sat in church and listened to the homily on Sunday mornings and would think, "Yes, that's it." Then I would be disappointed because it wasn't taken far enough. My turning point with organized religion revolved around a Parent/Teachers' meeting. A group of parents wanted the cafeteria reopened so the children could have hot lunches. The neighborhood was maturing; fewer children were attending parochial grade school. Money was not flowing in as it used to. The priest stated that the only way he could reopen the cafeteria was to receive federal aid and to do that the school would be required to take in a certain percentage of minorities. Then he said, "We don't want those kinds of people, now do we?" Well…he was a mere mortal and had not yet learned the lesson of accepting those who appear different from us, although he did preach the principles of love and respect for others every Sunday. What can I say?

As I was learning to work through my fears, my husband was growing more and more into his. Unfortunately, all his "what ifs" came true. I can hear Gram saying that we get what we focus on. We have a choice to awaken or be swallowed into oblivion by fear. The brave may not live forever, but the cautious don't live at all.

His was the fifth car waiting in line for the traffic light to change when a collision occurred ahead of him and brought a car crashing into his side. After a few weeks in a rehabilitation hospital, my husband was physically fine, but emotionally he discovered how your life could change in an instant. Realizing that one has no real control over his or her life terrified him to the depth of his being.

A little later, the company he worked for was involved in the longest strike in Erie history. Since he was an engineer in management, he continued to work. He and another man ran a machine that kept the company going during the eight months it took to reach a settlement. These two men became the sacrificial lambs to the union and were let go at the end of the strike. My husband couldn't believe this was the reward for all the work he had put in; for all the verbal abuse he took from the union workers. He never did get over his justified anger. He just couldn't move beyond it.

After that, he was unable to hold down a job for long. He became more insulated, more isolated from the world at large. He grew more and more into himself; communicating less and less with us. He only left the house to do grocery shopping or visit his family. We lost respect for each other… our harmony was no more. He turned against me…cut me out…blamed me for the pressure of a large mortgage. While his career went south, mine was climbing.

I finally gave him an either/or ultimatum. We either go to marriage counseling or else I'm out of here. Marriage counseling only works if both people want to work at changing what isn't working. He wouldn't do his homework. He thought nothing was wrong with him, if only I would change. He couldn't accept that I was changing…just not the way he wanted and I couldn't accept his refusal to change in order to save our marriage.

Through Gram's teachings, I learned that the only person you can control/change is yourself. In my first marriage, I allowed myself to be a battered wife. After ten years of abuse, I said "no more." Two failed marriages were not what I planned in my life's agenda…

After the separation, he stalked me. He thought there was somebody else. There wasn't. I would awaken to find him standing beside my bed at four in the morning. The locks to the house were changed several times, but he always managed to gain entry. Our security was seized by his insecurity. This took its toll on us. We had a hard time sleeping. The outside lights were kept on all night. We awoke to every little noise. We didn't know what he wanted…or wanted to do to us. The girls were afraid of what he would do to me. He wanted me to suffer for leaving him, but he didn't notice it was the girls who were suffering.

We were advised to move. This we did, only to discover he was coming into our new home. Once again, we had the locks changed to no avail. Because I couldn't change his actions, I decided to change mine. I no longer changed the locks. He needed to see for himself that there was nobody else. Maybe then, he would stop.

After the separation, he did get a job out-of-town for awhile but ended up coming back to Erie. It took two years for the divorce to become final. Throughout it all, the girls felt as if he were not only rejecting me but them as well. The loss of the father they once knew and still loved would weigh upon them forever.

Chapter 10

Nineteen ninety-five was a year packed full of learning and spiritual growth with Twylah as my teacher/mentor/friend. I loved making the one-and-a half-hour trek from Erie to the reservation. Each trip was a delicious adventure, as I never knew who would be there or what would take place. As I took the right hand turn off Route 20 onto Route 438, I could always feel the subtle change in energy. If someone should cover my eyes and ask where we were, I swear I would be able to tell. The landscape of the reservation looked like any other rural back road. We passed by modest older homes and house trailers displaying small vegetable gardens. Kids played outside and laundry dried on the line. Further on, we passed the usual white clapboard country church complete with gravel parking lot.

Pulling into Gram's driveway, I would sneak a peek into the small kitchen window at the back of her house to catch a glimpse of who was in attendance. The kitchen was the heartbeat of her home where everyone gathered. Parking the car, I filled with anticipation at seeing Gram and being able to, once more, walk the land that seemed to bring healing.

Susan and I never arrived empty handed. We always brought along food that Susan prepared for all present. We brought cookies, either homemade or from "The Ole Sweet Shope." Their chocolate chip cookies are out of this world because they are made from real butter and big chunks of good quality chocolate, not the usual small chips. Oh, how Gram loved cookies, especially the fruit filled ones! Upon arrival, I always sought out the Rainbow vacuum cleaner and proceeded to help clean the main level of the house. At the end of our visit, we always left some wrinkled green frog skins (money) to assist in obtaining whatever was needed.

Twylah was known as the "Pen and Paper Grandmother." Even though her teachings on how to live life in a harmonious way with each other and with nature are based on stories and experiences from her Seneca heritage, they apply to all cultures.

We would be sitting around her kitchen table drinking coffee and chatting away on some trivial topic when Twylah would walk into the room and say, "Now looky here, get out a pen and paper, I want to show you something. Now write down the word TRUST vertically on your paper. Okay, now think of a word for each letter and write it down." The next hour or so would center on a lesson involving trust. Gram ended the lesson by saying, "We must learn to say trust instead of hope. HOpe has a big hole in the middle in which the best of intentions can fall through. Trust contains the word US…you and me…together we can accomplish anything."

Her lessons always seemed very simple, but they managed to subtlety change us inside, to awaken an inner truth. Twylah was taught that we have all the answers inside us, we just have to bring them forth…to remember… to know…to understand.

Gram's birthday was in December. I loved giving her presents slanted towards her gentle femininity. One year, I gave her a basket full of nail polish and other assorted bottles of gook for her hands. I also gave her a card that read something to the extent of a mature woman is like an antique chifforobe because eventually her chest falls into her drawers or similar wording equally silly. She had a great sense of humor and loved a good laugh. Oh, how her eyes sparkled when she laughed. Twylah would state, "It's healthy to smile because it releases energy that gets stuck. That's why a hearty laugh is the best medicine."

During my years of travel to the reservation, much unrest took place with the state of New York trying to impose taxes upon the reservation and inter-tribal concerns surrounding the issue of allowing gambling casinos on Native land. Some events even made national network news. There was a short period when non-natives were not welcome on the land. I tried to steer clear of the political issues, as my reason for being on the land was to gain wisdom on life. People from around the world flocked to her house for this same guidance. I was fortunate to meet many of them and to develop lasting friendships with a few.

When initiated into the Seneca Indian Historical Society Wolf Clan Teaching Lodge (SIHS) Gra, along with the help of Spirit, gave me the name of Gonohdo, *She Who Knows*. It was an unexpected name to receive as I felt I knew nothin'!

Overall, the best times at her house were when nobody else was present. That's when we would sit quietly in her living room and have the most amazing conversations. People tended to use her time and energy asking for guidance on their personal lives. I never did this. She didn't even know that since I had embraced the teachings, I had gotten divorced.

Gram often spoke of the Indian way of learning. She recalled, "I was taught to *ask* questions of the teacher, not to *answer* questions from your teacher." As I became more confident in my learning, I started to ask questions. I asked if the medicine name given to me was a name I was to *become*, not where I was right now. "Yes, Jean," she replied. I mentioned that Susan and our friend, Eileen, were also given medicine names that started with "She Who" as Grams did (*She Whose Voice Rides the Winds*). Gram told me, "The people who were given this prefix are the initiators, the activators of Truth. They are the people who will *learn* the Truth, *live* the Truth, and *share* the Truth with others so Truth can continue. They are the teachers who will spread the Truth. Truth is all there is in accordance with Nature, which is all the forces of the Uniworld melded into one for survival." It took me many years to just begin to understand what this meant and I'm still learning!

I once revealed to Gram that I felt such an intimate connection with her. "How so?" she inquired. I replied that it was not like the connection of a blood sister or daughter but deeper, even deeper than a soul connection. I had a hard time getting the next words out because I felt unworthy to put myself on the same level as Gram. Continuing I said, "It's as if we are somehow twins…no deeper than that…" I just couldn't find the right words to explain what I felt inside. I also relayed that although I had only been in Grandmother Sara Smith's presence a few times, I also felt this same connection with her. Twylah replied, "Sara and I are sisters, but not sisters of blood. You are right in feeling the three of us are connected. We come from the same mold; we are of the same weave…cloth."

A time came when she patiently told me, "Now listen, I've taught you everything I know; it's now time for you to go out and share with others." In a procrastinating whiny voice I said, "I can't speak the Seneca words you use; I'm not comfortable using the medicine wheel to teach others." Gram countered back with, "Jean, Truth is Truth. I use my Seneca heritage to share the Truth, you must find your own way; you don't have to emulate mine."

I replied, "I don't feel as if I have the whole puzzle put together yet." Remember that crystal boundary of mine; I must have the complete picture before proceeding. I asked if other teachers had other knowledge. With great patience she said, "Jean, what you are looking for is right in front of your eyes. When you recognize it, you will say, 'Geez, is that all it is, it's that simple!' "

Gram confirmed that we came into this Earthwalk to remember how to be one with the Creator. Through learning *my* personal Pathway of Peace, I discovered that one of the gifts I entered this Earthplane with is the ability to attract and release what I need/don't need to learn. Also, by listening to the silent stillness within myself, I will learn how to share the Truth with others, so they may gain the knowledge to become whole. This is how I will honor my own personal Truths.

Gram told me, "Truth comes in nuggets. If you read a book and there is one passage…one sentence…one phrase…that resonates within your heart, that *you* know is Truth, then it was worth reading the whole book." The same goes for a church service, a lecture, a chance conversation with a stranger.

I learned that life is always a matter of balance. How can we enjoy the light if there is no darkness to compare it with? Grams stated, "Darkness is just the absence of light…of Truth." After rain come the flowers. The closer we get to Truth/Light the more obstacles/challenges are put in our way…a wall… to test our resolve of becoming whole. The brighter the light—the deeper the darkness—the balance. As humans, we must learn to live *in* balance. Gram said, "When our bodies are out of balance we become diseased, at *dis-ease* with ourselves."

Gram loved to play with words. One day we got into a discussion of the devil. She said, "The meaning of evil is not to live life fully. Evil spelled backwards is LIVE. It is *fear* that keeps us from living because we don't listen within…with our inner *ear.*"

I have tried to teach my children, through a variety of lessons, that fear is like a cloud in the sky. When you look at it from the ground, it appears to be solid for it can block out the sun…the light. Nevertheless, when you're in an airplane, you can fly right through it. We must learn to not let fear stop us. That, indeed, we can pass right through it like a plane passing through a cloud and come out into the light on the other side.

It was one of those special times when we were alone in the house. I asked Gram her opinion on the situation in the Middle East. I said there must be something in the land that causes this disruption of energy…that people can't seem to live in peace in that area. It seems there have always been disputes throughout the ages and that several religions claim ownership of the land. Instead of bringing nations together, it seems to keep them apart. Her reply surprised me. She responded with, "Remember the balance of all things. It's better to keep the disruption in one area so it doesn't come over to us (to the U.S.)."

Journal Entry–May 19, 1995

Tuesday, Susan and I went to visit Twylah. Gram is definitely one of my spiritual mentors. She reacted very differently towards me this visit, asking my opinion, and respecting my answers.

As Susan and I sat at the kitchen table with some other visitors, the discussion got around to men. Two women were yakking away, not paying much attention to the rest of us when Twylah said, "Now be quiet for a minute and listen to what Jean is saying. A lot of wisdom is coming out of her mouth." I think it was more hands-on experience then wisdom! Later that day she asked if I would help her with her weekend intensives–to teach the Pathway of Peace. Sue volunteered to cook and clean, but I suggested that both of us teach the Pathway of Peace together.

When we told Gram we were planning on going to the Peace Elders Council to be held in Puerto Rico in November, she said, "Good, you can do some teaching for me." I felt honored that Twylah held me in respect, but I am also afraid that I couldn't live up to her expectations.

I know this must sound so shallow, but at the last minute, we decided not to travel to Puerto Rico. I didn't think I could make it sleeping in a tent in rain forest terrain. Where would I plug in my curling iron? The vision of the mud at the Women's Council ran through my head and I didn't want to go through that again. Guess I didn't live up to her expectations…this time.

Journal Entry–May 28, 1995

What a weekend this has been! Sue and I went to Twylah's yesterday. It turned out to be more then we could have imagined.

I brought along a log about two feet long which was gifted to me by my supervisor. I wanted to get Twylah's opinion of it. My supervisor was walking in the woods when there it was, right smack in the middle of the path. She said she thought of me right away. The log was unusual as it was stripped bare of its bark. Beaver had chewed on both ends and the middle. Each end was chewed into a point and the middle was chewed into a "V."

Susan and I thought we were going to help Twylah teach an *Intensive* to a family of four. Boy, did we think wrong! When we arrived, the house was full of people Twylah had called in to participate in a pipe ceremony. Since it was a ceremony, Susan and I thought we would not be able to take part since we are non-native. Gram said, "Scoot out there with the others."

We gathered in a patch of cool refreshing grass behind the teaching lodge. As we sat in circle, I placed the log at my feet. Roland, and his wife, Linda, performed the ceremony. Susan and I felt privileged to be a part of this ceremony, to bring the pipe ceremony back to the peoples of the East. The Seneca are the keepers of the western door. They wanted to do the ceremony on Twylah's land because of her standing in the Seneca Nation.

Although we were not allowed to smoke the pipe ourselves, Roland did pick up my log, held it above his head, said a prayer and proceeded to blow smoke all around it. I cried during the ceremony, as I knew a great Truth was taking place.

A few hours later we all sat around outside while Roland started teaching about choice. I questioned if indeed we had choice or if we are chosen. What if we don't want the responsibility? He replied, "At some level we do make the choice and some of us indeed have a greater responsibility placed on us." Linda said she would speak to me later on this.

After talking a while longer, Susan and I went into the kitchen to prepare dinner. Before long, I was called out to the teaching lodge to escort the youngest of the family through initiation into the Wolf Clan Teachings. Susan continued to prepare the meal. Is this a sign that I am truly a teacher for the Wolf Clan Teaching Lodge?

Linda approached me after dinner and asked, "Why were you crying earlier?" I told her it's because I feel I will have a great mission ahead of me and I don't know if I am up to the responsibility. I told her how I had watched her and her husband and how they seemed to fit so well together–that is what I wanted and needed in my life if I am to accomplish my mission. I told her

I had been married twice and somehow what they have together eludes me. She responded by saying, "Don't worry, once you accept your mission, he will come along." I replied, "I always believed he had to be in place before I could start my mission." Linda responded back with, "You are right, it is too great a task both mentally and physically to accomplish without a mate by your side." She said that both she and Roland had been married twice before also. "We don't always agree, but we do honor and respect each other. Don't worry, yours is on his way."

Journal Entry–July 17, 1995

I had a reading done tonight. I was told I am a message bearer to others. I help to make things happen for them by what I say. I bring people of many groups and cultures together, that I am a resource center or network for them. She also said that I am balanced. People at work will try to pull at me, but I am to remain indifferent—and only say words of peace. I am there for their healing and I am to be detached. I am to treat everyone the same. She said it is good I am with Twylah—perhaps I will write about her teachings.

Journal Entry–July 31, 1995

What a weekend with Twylah. She sure does keep you hopping!

It seemed I was going morn-to-night, from the time Susan and I got there on Friday until we left Sunday afternoon. We helped Gram conduct an *Intensive* and we helped her build a new wheel on the Keys of Time. We also helped write a step-by-step process for personal gifts based on the Cycles of Truth and the person's name and birth date.

Three women from England were present. Two traveled together and were from northern England. I ended up inviting them to my house for the following weekend. The other woman, Janet, grew up in the states, and met her British husband at her place of work in New York City. They married and now live north of London. Janet and I must have a spiritual bond as we hit it off right away.

Journal Entry–September 20, 1995

Susan, my friend, Naomi, and I went to visit Twylah. It was an enjoyable day.

While getting dressed this morning I heard a faint scraping against the wall behind my bed. I called Melanie in to see if she heard it. She discovered a butterfly caught between the headboard and the wall. It finally came out and landed on my rock from Helgafel, a sacred mountain in Iceland. Mel and I managed to steer the butterfly to an open window so it could fly away.

(My daughter-in-law, Saeunn, hails from Iceland and their wedding took place in her hometown of Stykklsholmur. While there, I climbed the sacred mountain near her hometown and brought the rock back as a reminder."

Upon relating the story to Gram, she gave her interpretation, "The butterfly needed you to help it continue its journey. It had to get out of the crazy energy that was outside. You aided it, the rock gave it stability, and then it was released to continue on its journey to complete its mission."

Being with Twylah, in her home, was such an interesting period in my life. I was learning so much from her and her wonderful land. It was becoming harder and harder to break away and come back to my mundane life. Because of my family and work responsibilities, I couldn't stay for days or weeks on end like others did; it was a weekend here, a night there. I knew she was looking for assistance with the teachings, but the timing was not right for me. Not now.

Chapter 11

*A*h, Coyote's at it again! Coyote sits in the South on my personal medicine wheel. I was taught that the South is the position that protects the child within and guides you on who to trust. The coyote is the trickster. Its medicine produces laughter and joking so that new viewpoints may be obtained. Or, on the other hand, is it Grandmother Sara's influence? Remember, all her teachings are oral in the traditional way, so we remember only what we need. Whatever the reason, the journals covering several years in my life have disappeared. I'll have to recall Wolf Song and the events leading up to it from memory. This shouldn't be hard as it is indelibly etched in my soul.

Wolf Song VI was to be held on Mary Thunder's ranch in Tyler, Texas. Thunder is part Irish, Cheyenne, and adopted Lakota. She became a Peace Elder at the first Peace Elder's Council–Wolf Song and then went on to host the second one.

I arrived at the reservation to find everyone abuzz about the upcoming event. Who was going? How would they get there? Who would speak? What was to be Gram's message? When I left, it seemed all the arrangements had been made. Gram and her son, Jim, would travel to Texas via a RV with Karen as the driver. Karen had been staying on the land, helping Twylah with the teachings. Twy was now 84.

The next time I went up to Gram's, things were all a twitter. It seemed nobody at the res would be attending as their plans had fallen through. How would Twylah's message get there? Who would present it? Dumb naïve me.... or was it that trickster Coyote? Having never attended a Council, I had no idea what it encompassed. I told Gram that if she couldn't get anyone else, I would attend and present her message. She asked me to come back Tuesday night and she would sit with me to prepare. This I did. I left her house with charts in hand (remember she is the Pen and Paper Grandmother) and the oral story of the Peacemaker's birth. Her last words to me were, "Now don't forget to begin by telling the story of the Peacemaker." The Natives' Peacemaker is akin to Jesus and was sent by the Maker of Men to spread Peace among all the Nations.

Off I flew to the Lone Star State, lugging a large suitcase, rolled up charts, and Laurie's big tent; the same one we used for the Women's Council. My friend, Naomi, gifted me with a book to read on the plane entitled *A Million Visions of Peace*, written and illustrated by children and edited by Andrew Tubesing and Jennifer Garrison. It's filled with such lovely heartwarming young wisdom, but it's also disturbing. Our children are frightened. I encourage all of you to read it

Arriving in Austin late Thursday afternoon, I rented a car, and set off for another small dot on the map–Tyler, Texas. Unfortunately, unlike the last time I traveled to a small dot on the map, there was no friendly AmyLee at the door to greet me. After driving for several hours on a deserted highway to the middle of nowhere, I arrived at the ranch in darkness.

I knocked on the door of Thunder's house and reluctantly was let in. I quickly introduced myself and said I was sent by Twylah to help with the preparations and to deliver her message. They looked at me as if I were crazy. Me deliver Twylah's message? Who was this woman? They never heard of me. Seeing the look of disbelief on their faces, I wondered, "Didn't Twylah let them know I was coming?"

I reluctantly took a seat in the background as Thunder was having a last minute organizational meeting. It appeared they didn't have enough hands to complete all that needed to be done before the start of the event. After listening for a while, I reminded them I was there to help, just let me know how. I was ignored and not given an assignment even though 109 elders were to start arriving tomorrow.

Since I was too travel weary to set-up my tent at ten o'clock at night (midnight my time), I was graciously invited to share a tent with two other women attending the event. We walked through the darkness to their canvas home. Upon pushing through the flap with my large suitcase, I realized that I would be one too many people to occupy this small space. So, off I went to search for a hotel, never to spend a whole night on the land.

Friday morning I returned to the ranch and walked into the middle of a discussion on picking some people up at the Houston airport. There was only one vehicle at their disposal and it didn't have enough room to fit all three people and their luggage. Dumb naïve me…here comes Coyote again. I volunteered to drive my rental, not realizing that Houston was almost four hours away. Thunder took me up on my offer, but she instructed the other driver that the elders were to ride with her. What is this? Do I have cooties on me? Am I unclean? Just what did I do to deserve this treatment? After all, I was good enough to use my gas to pick-up one person…one person. I didn't understand.

When we arrived at the designated terminal hours later, I immediately spotted a man and a woman standing outside the entrance. As we walked past them towards the doors, I caught the woman's eye and we smiled at each other. The driver of the van couldn't locate the people we were supposed to retrieve. She said, "I'm going to call the ranch to see if they have been in communication." As we approached the pay phones (no cell phones back then), the same man and woman were at the bank of phones. I approached them with, "Excuse me, are you Jacki and Steve?" Sure enough they were. I wondered why the other driver didn't intuitively know as I had.

As Jacki and Steve were piling into the van, they disclosed they were famished and asked if we could stop to eat somewhere on the way back to the ranch. We ended up at a Taco Bell where we all sat at the same table, talked together, and laughed together. Jacki told me about her pending divorce. (I know…I know, I just met this woman and she tells me her personal story. As strange as it may seem, this happens to me all the time. I can be sitting on a plane beside a stranger and they start to tell me intimate details about their life. They find me trustworthy enough to open up…it's the healer in me.) As we were walking back to the car, I informed Jacki, "I have a present for you." (Now I know why I had brought along a medicine pouch made up for me by a friend when I was going through my divorce. It was time to pass it on. Jacki, Steve, and I became friends at this event and remain so to this day. So much for trying to keep me away from the elders!)

After dropping off my passenger, I returned to the hotel and put in a call to Twylah to relay what was happening in regards to whether I would be allowed to speak. I informed Twy that I am not recognized as her representative. She advised, "Do not push your presence upon Thunder. Stand a short distance away, but remain in her line of vision so she is aware of you." I followed Gram's instructions.

Saturday morning arrived and the opening of Wolf Song commenced out in the open air under the brilliant blue cloudless Texas sky. I only knew two people out of the hundreds that attended, Grandma Sara Smith and Karen.

The Council fire was ignited and the drum that kept the heartbeat of the Council had begun. Both would be kept going day and night until the Council ended. Praises and prayers went out to Twylah and her grandfather, Moses Shongo. My eyes grew misty at the mention of their names.

It is now Saturday afternoon and I'm still not informed if I am to speak. I searched the land for a spot away from everything and said a prayer. After lunch, I went back to the hotel and put in a call to Twy. I felt like a wolf with my tail between my legs, as if I wouldn't be able to accomplish what she had sent me to do, that I had let her down. Her response was, "Jean, keep your eye on Mary, the more she denies your presence the more confused and disorganized she will become." That's exactly what appeared to be happening for the rest of the afternoon…for the rest of the event. Although I had never met Mary before, she seemed out of sorts to me, very "un-with-it."

For some reason, I *was* allowed to sit in the inner circle with the elders, while all the other attendees had to stay behind a ring of hay bales used to separate the two groups. But wasn't Wolf Song about unity, not separation?

Needing a break, I went back to the hotel in the early evening and put in yet another call to Gram. I informed her that I still was not given the go-ahead but felt her speech had changed. Our conversation consisted of what I felt led to say. All that came out of her mouth was, "Yes Jean, yes Jean," giving voice of approval to everything. In looking back, I think what audacity I had to inform Twylah HER message had changed!

Returning to the ranch in the evening, I felt compelled to accompany Karen in a sweat lodge ceremony being held on the land. I had done a sweat lodge a few years ago that left a lasting impact on me. Although it was a positive experience, I can't say I'm fond of them. The Inipe Ceremony (sweat lodge) is made up of four rounds of prayers and chanting which results in spiritual renewal and purification of body, mind, soul, and spirit.

Gram once told me, "Women don't need to cleanse themselves via this way; we cleanse our bodies every month with our Moontime." AmyLee said there are different medicines for different parts of the Earth and the medicine only works correctly in that location. I always associated the Inipe Ceremony with the Plains Indians, although similar ceremonies are held throughout the world.

In any event, I felt I must do this sweat with Karen to show our unity with Gram. We entered the lodge in appropriate dress (no pants or shorts allowed for women) and sat in the last circular row. Some younger men were sitting in front of us, shielding us from the direct heat produced by hot rocks sprinkled with water. After round one, four of the men left. Although this gave us more room, it exposed us directly to the intense rising heat. Having difficulty breathing, I decided to lay on the ground in a fetal position, closer to the Earth where it was a tad bit cooler. The next thing I knew, Karen gave me a nudge, saying it was time to go, the ceremony was over. I told her I must have conked out, I don't remember going through the other rounds.

The last thing I remembered was the sound of the rattle. I don't recall the name of the Native man who conducted the sweat, but I do remember him saying his rattle was a medicine rattle that had been handed down through the generations. I will never forget its magical sound. Although the rattle never physically left his hand, its sound did travel to each individual in that dome, going up and over each head and shoulder then moving on to the next person. As it approached Karen, the sound traveled up and over her head, then proceeded to come down to where I was lying on the ground. I heard/felt it travel the length of my body and then go on the next person. This is the last thing I remember before Karen shook me.

With the Sunday morning dawn came the last hours of Wolf Song and I still had not received permission to speak. As the procession was heading towards the wood skeleton of a teaching lodge for morning ceremony, I approached Grandmother Sara and asked if she could intervene, speak to the master of ceremonies on my behalf. She said, "This is not my way. My way is to conduct a prayer with tobacco." So here in a water-starved field that was being used as a temporary parking lot, with the glaring Texas sun shining down on us, Grandmother Sara spread her prayer bundle out on the hood of a pick-up truck and conducted a tobacco prayer to Great Mystery. When finished she advised, "You must accept whatever happens." I assured her I would.

As I sat in circle listening to the Elders speak, the final few hours were fast approaching. I was thinking about what Sara had said when one of Mary's helpers appeared behind me and said, "You will speak shortly." I noticed that only Peace Elders spoke and asked if I were to be made one. Was it Coyote, that trickster…again? Why did I ask as I really didn't care? She responded, "Do you want to be one?" I replied that one does not ASK for such an honor, that it is bestowed upon them. She left and came back a short time later announcing, "You will be made a Peace Elder in about five minutes and then you will speak right after." Oh my, why did they spring this on me at the last moment giving me no time to make the necessary preparations that Twylah and I had discussed the previous night?

I had relayed to Twy that so far there was no mention of the children at this Council. I asked if I could use the book Naomi had given me as Twy's message for peace. I had selected passages from the book, actual words written by children expressing their thoughts/wants/wishes for peace. After reading the selections over the phone, Gram said, "Yes, Jean, by all means do so; it's a wonderful idea." As she talked, I could imagine her eyes sparkling and could hear the delight in her voice. I said it would be nice for the children on the land to be present to hear the message. She agreed.

I had made many friends at this event. Among them were Chris and Ceri from Great Britain. They were present to gather material for a documentary they were filming for the BBC on crystal skulls. Two of the skulls were present. They also wrote a book on this subject titled *The Mystery of the Crystal Skulls*. As I waited my anointing, I looked out and saw Chris and Ceri walking across the field towards the circle. I ran out and asked them to gather the children and bring them into the tent. I was about to speak and the children needed to be present. Just then, I was called back into the tent.

Standing on the speaking platform recounting the birth of the Peacemaker, I looked out across the field to see Chris and Ceri approaching with several children in tow. They each had two or three children linked to their hands, forming a moving chain of destiny that was fast approaching.

I followed up the Peacemaker's story with Twylah's approved selections from the book, thus giving voice to the children's words. The audience laughed at some of the passages while the Elders nodded in agreement with the innocent heartfelt statements.

Looking out across the grounds again, I saw more children running across the field. Unbeknownst to me, the security people had radioed on their walkie-talkies to call in the children from all over the ranch. What a wonderful site! It brought tears to my eyes as I asked the audience to look out and behold the future. As I continued, I noticed a mother coming forward with her weeks-old baby strapped to her chest. Later, she told me she wanted her child to be a part of this moment. People started moving up to sit on the hay bales used to delineate the inner circle of Elders from the rest of the participants. No longer was there a dividing line; all of us were equal in hearing the pleas of the children.

When I finished, the whole audience stood up and clapped. I didn't delude myself into believing the applause was for me personally, as I knew it was for the powerful message I was chosen to deliver. I was just the messenger. As I turned around to leave the stage, what a surprise it was to see it filled with children eating cookies that one of the male Elders was passing out. I learned later that I might have unintentionally stolen some of Mary's "Thunder" by bringing the children on stage. They were to parade into the circle later in the day displaying pictures they had drawn. The cookies were for then. With my mission complete, I could now leave.

The following Tuesday I was called up to the res, not by phone but by the internal network Gram uses when she wants to see you. Upon arriving, she promptly separated me from the others. She led me into her private room, closed the door, and sat me down on a chair. She then bent down and took both my hands in hers, looked me in the eyes, and with a big smile said, "Jean, I am so proud of you. My phone started ringing right after you finished speaking." The master of ceremonies had telephoned saying what a great job I had done. I couldn't believe it as he was one of the people giving me gruff. She said her phone had constantly been ringing off the hook about the presentation. In the end, all that mattered to me was that Gram was happy.

I found out that all kinds of people were showing up at the ranch claiming Gram had sent them to deliver her message, people known in Native American circles. I was an unknown. Why should they believe that Twylah, the originator and spiritual leader of this event, had sent me? Was Mary Thunder on the phone daily with Twylah as I had been? Didn't she ask Gram who was to give her message? Where was the communication? Perhaps Gram sent us all and then sat back to see who would succeed.

Chapter 12

The space of time between Wolf Song VI and Wolf Song VII held in August of 1997 would forever leave an indelible imprint on all the existing members of the Seneca Indian Historical Society and the Wolf Clan Teaching Lodge.

Gram's son, Jim, lived in a house a scant 15 or so feet from hers. Whenever anyone would visit Twylah, it was only a matter of minutes before he would stroll into the kitchen to see what was happening. Jim was to be the one to take over the teachings where Gram would leave off. He was tall and lanky with very dark black hair and Gram's sparkling eyes. He held a zest for life that couldn't be contained.

In March of '97, Gram's internal network called to me again, so I placed a call to the res. I was surprised when her daughter answered the phone. She told me that Jimmy had died the night before, his house had caught fire and he was unable to escape. I offered my condolences and immediately said a prayer upon hanging up. I stayed away from the funeral to show respect for the family; it was their private time. I was told Gram was having a very hard time accepting his death and that she was very, very weak. After the funeral, she went to live with her other son, Bob, in Florida.

Just like that…things changed. Gram was no longer just one-hour and thirty-minutes away. My prayer was that she would grow strong and return to the reservation. After all, generations of her family had lived on that land. That land that was so special to me, that land that offered repose to all who set foot on it. She was born in that house. How could she leave it? Such were the mundane selfish thoughts running through my mind, but in my heart I understood how unbearable it would be for her to see empty space where her future once lived. Unbeknownst to me at the time, I would suffer a similar tragedy seven years later.

In August, Wolf Song VII had traveled back to Twylah's homeland. The event wasn't well organized; everyone was still in shock over Jim's death and Gram's move to Florida. These changes imprinted a wound on the land that couldn't be ignored.

My friends and I arrived early to help with last minute details. We were in charge of registration and pitched our tent by the driveway to greet all who entered onto the land.

The opening ceremony was about to start when it was realized that the Wolf Song Council Drum that had kept the heartbeat at the previous Councils was no more. It had been stored in Jim's house. What was to be done? I offered up my small hand-held drum purchased at the Wolf Song in Texas. It was customized to my request with brown paint to form bear paw prints making a path across the drum on one side and wolf paw prints on the other. Brown is the color of knowing, the color associated with my spiritual name of *She Who Knows*. I wanted to keep the drum plain and simple...like Gram's teachings. I was told that not any drum could be used; it has to be made in a medicine manner. When I replied that Tar Water had made my drum, the conversation ended. About an hour later, a man approached me and said, "It has been requested that your drum be used to keep the heartbeat of Wolf Song VII." It was.

In the fall, Bob made a trip back to the reservation to move the remainder of Twylah's belongings. I called and asked if I could meet him at the house. For some reason I wanted to meet this other son, to see if he "stood tall" and to hear how Gram was doing from his lips as there were many rumors circulating.

Bob turned out to be a delightful man with a sense of humor like his mother's. He is tall in stature like his younger brother and has curly silver hair. As we walked the land, we talked of his family, his heritage, and his future. It was to be the last time I would sit in the teaching lodge, a sacred space where I had learned so much about myself and met so many wonderful allies who were on the same path. It brought tears to my eyes to say goodbye to this peaceful patch of earth. Bob inherited Gram's mission of passing on her teachings of living in Truth...the cycle continues, generation to generation.

Later in the year, I traveled to Florida to help celebrate Gram's 85th birthday. My friend, Eileen, lives in central Florida and came up for the day.

Eileen is also a member of the Wolf Clan Teaching Lodge. The three of us had a delightful visit, but the phone continuously rang with people calling from all over the world to deliver their birthday wishes. All that conversation tired Twylah. I can understand why their phone number had to change routinely; it would be like that each and every day!

Isn't it odd how life events can hit you smack in the face and bingo…your destiny changes? This happened to my second husband with his car accident and now it was happening to Bob. Soon it would happen to me.

Chapter 13

In looking back, I believe my Earthwalk changed with the birth of my fourth child. I was thirty-four years old, attending Penn State Erie and enjoying the experience. This was my second marriage. I had two boys, Ed and Wayne, to my first husband and a girl, Le'Anne, to my second husband. He was feeling a little insecure about this whole school thing and announced he would like another child.

To appease him, I became pregnant. Unfortunately, I had a miscarriage two months into the pregnancy. Although several weeks of school were compromised, I still managed to pull B's in all my subjects. A short time later, I became pregnant once again.

This pregnancy zapped my energy. I was now thirty-five and was having difficulty finding enough time in the day to run the house, take care of the children, do my schoolwork, and give my husband attention. Something had to give...reluctantly I gave up school.

Melanie was born during a full moon. My water broke around 11 PM on March 19, but I didn't go into labor. The next morning around 8 AM the doctor took me into the hospital and induced labor, still I wasn't dilating. It became late afternoon; I became extremely exhausted and began to doubt the doctor's judgment.

You see, when I was six months pregnant with Le'Anne, I had a horrible experience. I was told the intense pain I was experiencing was a bladder infection. Finally, after three days of excruciating pain, I was to have exploratory surgery to see what was causing the pain. We were shocked to find out my appendix had broken! Now, you know why I questioned the doctor's judgment this time around.

Labor was not progressing. The doctor said if nothing happened within the next two hours he would have to do a C-section. I asked why he was waiting, that I was in so much pain it would be better to die then to continue in labor. A half-hour later, they were wheeling me into the delivery room. Melanie finally came into this world at 7:13 PM. I always said if she had been the first instead of the last, I might not have had any more children!

As I was being wheeled to my room after delivery, a nurse passed me in the hallway with Melanie bundled up in a heated bed. Next to her side was the placenta—in a plastic bag. This struck me as very strange. Even though I asked several times, nobody ever explained why.

For the first three months of Melanie's life, I had to be the one to hold her and give her love, comfort, and reassurance that this Earthplane is all right. If anyone tried to hold her, she would cry until I came to her rescue. I remember visiting some relatives in Indiana who owned a restaurant. While we went off to dinner, the wife stayed behind to take care of Melanie so I could have a relaxing dinner. We returned to find a look of extreme fatigue on her face. She stated Melanie had cried the whole time. When I retrieved Melanie from her arms, she instantly stopped crying. Go figure!

"Mellie," my pet name for her, had the usual happy toddler life. Her two brothers and sister played with her and taught her the things they felt were important like how to sit underneath the kitchen table; however, they forgot to teach her how to crawl out. They made fortresses out of couch pillows and blankets and rode sleds down the small hill in our backyard. It was a joyous time for all of us!

In kindergarten, she had a series of throat infections and the doctor recommended removing her adenoids. She refused to go into surgery without her favorite stuffed dog, Lazy. When she was a year old, we vacationed at Hershey Park and her father won it for her. She has slept with it every night since and wouldn't let go of it now. The nurses had no choice but to carefully wrap it in plastic and lay it by her side.

When she awoke from the surgery she asked, "What's my name this time?" At the time, I thought it was a strange question to ask. We took her home that afternoon and as evening approached she started running a very high temperature. Not wanting to keep everyone up, I decided to have her sleep on the couch and I slept on the floor next to her. Sometime during the night, she sat straight up and starting screaming, "I want my mother." I told her I was right beside her. She said, "No, you're not my mother, I want my mother." As she talked, her voice grew fainter and fainter as if she were going farther and farther away, out of the room, out of the house. Then she started talking in several foreign languages, none of which I understood, but they sounded as if they were really old languages, perhaps no longer spoken. This really freaked me out and I was getting scared.

She started making a cross on my face, moving from my forehead to my chin and then on to each cheek the while rapidly counting, "One, two, three, four; one, two, three, four." Then she stroked the side of my face, saying, "I love you so much" with all the intensity of a man in war longing for his love back home. While all this was taking place, her eyes were open, but they had a blank expression, as if *my* Melanie was no longer inside that body. I started asking her to follow the sound of my voice; that I love her and Jesus loves her. Please come back to the sound of my voice. Once again, I saw the light within her eyes and she was back into her body. She lay back down and went to sleep. In the morning, she remembered nothing. A trip back to the doctor revealed the high fever was due to tonsillitis. Dumb shit! Why didn't he take those out, too?

Before the operation, Melanie was a very delicate, sensitive child. She would get nervous about the littlest things, for instance, if I raised my voice or corrected one of the other children. It always seemed to me that her soul was too delicate for this Earthplane. It's as if she possessed the energy frequency of an angel and the Earth's frequency was just too heavy for her.

After the fever subsided, it seemed her personality changed overnight. No longer was she a sweet sensitive child. She became challenging, pugnacious. She would give me a look as if to say, "I am so much smarter than you. Who are you to provide direction to me?" She kept this combative attitude for the rest of her life.

A few months later Melanie wanted to discuss her early years...pre-surgery. She inquired, "What was I like as a baby? What did I play with? Can I see my baby pictures?" We would sift through the pictures as if she couldn't get enough. She wanted to know where each picture was taken and if she was happy then. She just didn't seem to remember her earlier years, not even by reviewing the photo albums.

This period always stuck with me. It followed me throughout her childhood. I couldn't erase it from my mind. I had always wondered what happened that night but didn't know who to approach about it. I didn't want people to think I was some kind of a weirdo. Anyway, most people would say she was hallucinating because of the high fever, but I knew differently.

Because of the change in personality, I feared another soul had taken over her body when she was too weak to resist. This was not the Melanie I knew pre-surgery. A mother knows. After her passing, I finally decided to talk to a spiritual counselor about it.

The physic explained that I was correct in that a change had occurred. However, it was not another soul that had taken over her body, but another aspect of Melanie's soul. This aspect could handle the hard lessons that were to come. The other aspect would not have been able to do that. This rang true within my heart and gave me some solace. I always worried about the soul of the baby that I birthed. I didn't want to think of her as being erased, snubbed out by a stronger force.

We lived in a modest house on a city block that contained three houses on one side of the street and an empty field on the other side. The lack of houses limited the amount of social interaction. Mel developed a very close friendship with Steven, the boy next door. His sister was around Le'Anne's age and the four of them always played together, ate together, and slept at each other's houses. When it was time for Stephen to enter kindergarten, his parents decided to keep him back one year so he could be in the same class with Melanie. I think it had something to do with maturity and they felt Melanie would be a help to him. The two continued to be close friends for a couple more years until his macho policeman father decided his son shouldn't be playing with girls anymore. Therefore, Melanie was pushed aside. I know she didn't understand why Steven abandoned her. This must have broken her heart at such a young tender age, but she would never talk about it. It was her first rejection of love.

The years passed and Mel was around ten when she started talking about her friend from Jupiter. It seems he would visit her during the night and take her to Jupiter to play, or so she said. I chalked it up to a vivid imagination and would ask her questions about him. One day she announced, "He told me not to talk about him to anyone. It's my secret." Well, upon hearing this I, once again, started to freak out and sought an opinion on what to make of this. I was instructed to cleanse the house and especially her bedroom with either a smudge stick or a white candle. Not taking any chances, I did both. If it comes to a struggle with him over Melanie, I am to look him in the eyes and not look away. He must be the first one to back down or else my soul would be lost forever. I don't remember who gave me this advice or why I took it seriously, but I did. Something inside told me I should.

About a week later, in dreamtime, I awoke to see a small figure in a dark blue one-piece flight suit walking down the hallway towards my bedroom. I knew this was the moment I was to be tested. The small figure wore a matching tight-fitting hood over its face with slits in the material so only the eyes would show. I jumped out of bed and met him at the doorway, as I knew he shouldn't enter the bedroom. I threw him down onto the hall floor and sat on top of him, my legs straddling both sides of his body and my arms holding down his shoulders. As I tried to look him in the eyes, the slits closed. Then I woke up. Talk about a vivid imagination…except…a few weeks later I asked Mel about her friend and she replied, "He went away, he was not happy with what you did." I swear…I didn't share my dream with anyone!

Chapter 14

Le'Anne's Ataxia first pushed into the physical around 10 years of age. This was before they even had a name for it—that came in the middle nineties. Melanie would always make fun of Le; she would pick on her, be downright cruel enough to make Le cry, never realizing that she carried the same destructive gene.

It was the afternoon of Melanie's junior prom. Mel and her friends were driving away from the school grounds, leaving early to prepare for the big night. On the front yard of the school, a reenactment of a fatal car accident was taking place. It demonstrated what can happen on prom night due to reckless driving. The driver of the car Mel was in became distracted and hit the car in front of her. All the girls were wearing their seat belts, all except Melanie, who was sitting in the front passenger seat. She hit her head on the windshield and rode to the hospital in the ambulance that was a part of the demonstration. Ironically, a demonstration that was supposed to help save lives, instead, became the catalyst for Mel's life ending—for it was this head trauma that activated her Ataxia.

ATAXIA (A-tax-e-a). For me, it's a four-letter word. It has aliases OPCA (Olive ponto cerebellar ataxia) and SCA (Spino-cerebellar ataxia) with a number following. Each number stands for different forms that produce different symptoms. My daughters have SCA8, a slow progressive form inherited from their father. This particular neurodegenerative disease affects speech, walking, eye movements, hyper-reflexia, and classical symptoms found in the other numbered ataxias. Some carry this gene all their life and are not affected. It can be activated by a head trauma. The result is death, as there is no known cure at the present time. Symptoms can be treated as they come along, but there is no cure for the disease itself.

I was at work when the school called. Never in all the years my children were growing up did I get a call from school, so I knew it must be serious.

The caller stated that Mel was on her way to the hospital by ambulance; she had been in a car accident. I was told not to panic, that she was not badly hurt. Little did we know…

When I arrived at the hospital, a mere 13 blocks away, she was laying on a gurney in the emergency room. A red bump took center stage on her forehead. Otherwise, she seemed all right. The doctor wanted to take a CAT scan just to make sure. The results indicated that all was OK with the head trauma, but did I know her cerebellum was smaller than normal? An alarm went off in my gut. Oh no, so is Le'Anne's.

As the doctor was relaying this information, Mel interrupted to say that her father's cerebellum is also small. Upon contacting her father to make him aware of the accident, he confirmed Mel's statement. After consulting with a neurologist, all of us had blood work done for genetic testing. It took months for the results to come back and the death sentence handed down. It was confirmed that the three of them had SCA8. The experts believe it must have started with a mutant gene in their father since nobody else in either family showed any of the symptoms.

For all intent and purposes, Mel could have been the Prom Queen that night because all the attention was focused on her. Red was Mel's dominant color of the evening–the color of her dress, the color of her forehead–the color of faith in Twylah's teachings. Everyone inquired about how she was feeling, as the whole school knew of the accident. They also admired her dress, the one she was reluctant to wear. Mel bragged that even the snooty girls came up and told her how much they loved her dress. What was so special about it? First of all, it was a one of a kind; you wouldn't find anyone else at the Prom wearing this dress. It was a sample dress I picked up for a mere forty pounds in a secondhand shop in Bath, England. Mel didn't like the idea of secondhand, even though it was a sample dress and had never been worn. She didn't think it was still in style. Her tall elegant stature gained from learning correct posture in dance class combined with the elegant silky material of the dress made her a knockout, in more ways than one. She came home elated by all the attention she received. This high lasted for several weeks.

Chapter 15

Journal Entry–March 20, 1999

Things that are important to me: Today is Melanie's 18th birthday. The sun is shining. My spiritual friends. My husband is on his way to me.

Nineteen Ninety-Nine brought a lot of changes into my life and the lives of my two daughters. A year that should have been brimming with happy occurrences turned into a year of changing currents.

Life became more hectic. I had been on special assignment in Harrisburg for over a year and the weekly 12-hour round trip had taken its toll. It was difficult being separated from the girls three-and-a-half days a week. Although they had their father to watch over them, they needed me. After several trial and error living arrangements, they demanded to sleep in their own beds. They finally settled into a routine of going to their grandmother's house (where their father lived) after school and eating dinner. Then they would come home to do their homework, sleep in their own beds, and prepare for school in the morning.

Mel had dreams of being an English teacher, but since the divorce, her grades were slipping. There was nobody there to insure her homework was completed. I would call home only to have it be a one-way conversation. "Did you do your homework?" "Yes, Mom." "Are you keeping the house straightened?" "Yes, Mom." "Anything I need to know?" "No, Mom." Unfortunately, these answers were not the truth of what was happening in my absence. I felt they deliberately punished me by not keeping the house clean. I would drive home every Thursday night, mentally and physical depleted, to a house that looked as though a tornado had gone through. Dirty dishes and clothes were scattered throughout the house. Food wrappers were thrown on the floor. Not one dirty dish could find its way into the dishwasher. Damp, smelly towels were piled high on the bathroom floor.

Monday morning and all day Friday, I worked out of the Erie office. On the short drive to work each Friday, I would cry my eyes out and wonder, "How much longer can I do this?" The girls needed me…the house needed me…I needed me. I knew there was no future in Erie, not professionally and not personally. Seeing the blue calmness of the lake in the distance brought me comfort. The lake seduced me to leave Pittsburgh many years ago. When I drove down the hill towards work, I talked to the lake and told it how beautiful it was and how it brought pleasure to so many people. You see, Erie is a tourist town and has seven miles of sandy beaches in a park-like setting. It's great in the summer. Winter is another story! By the time I pulled into the parking lot at work, my tears had dried. The lake understood my plight and willingly absorbed my anguished tears.

Instead of the weekends being devoted to down time with the girls, we had to clean. When I asked why the house was such a mess, Mel would reply, "We aren't your maids." The only way I could get them to help was if I promised to take them somewhere with the stipulation that the house had to be cleaned first.

Working in Harrisburg wasn't a good situation, but I had to provide for the girls. I could see the handwriting on the wall that the regional office in Erie would soon be closing, consolidating with the Pittsburgh Regional Office. Their father was unable to work anymore and because of their health needs, we needed the security and benefits a state job provided. The responsibility of taking care of the girls' emotional, physical, and monetary needs was solely on my shoulders. I was spiritually weakening from the weighty pull of home responsibilities on one side and work responsibilities on the other.

I was spiritually out of balance and couldn't find my way back. I was solely in survival mode. Unfortunately, Gram's teachings were not in the forefront during this period. She was living in Florida and I had very little contact with her anymore. My spiritual needs became neglected. My whole life was devoted to the girls and work. Because I took no time for myself, I became emotionally, physically, and spiritually depleted; a robot going through the motions of living. There was no joy, just feelings of despair.

It was over two years after the divorce before dating became a viable option. I only dated on the weekends the girls visited their father and never brought anybody home. I didn't want to be one of those women who brought home a string of men as I felt I wouldn't be a good role model for them. It would most likely take a long string of men before I would find the right one for me. No settling this time…no taking the easy way out…which never ended up being easy. This time, I would do the work needed to find the right man for me. And believe me, it is work!

I was about to give up when a gentleman from Virginia entered my life via the Internet in 1998. A retired Coast Guard Aviator, Don, was also looking for a life partner. Gram said that one of the criteria I should use to measure a potential husband is to ask myself, "Does he stand tall? I don't mean tall as in stature, but does he stand tall in his Truth?" Don was certainly a man who knew his Truth and lived it. He walked his talk. After a lifetime of disappointing relationships, I found a man I could respect and love.

At the end of an eight-month courtship, we married in March 1999. We decided to marry in a small town close by Harrisburg that was established with the help of Don's ancestors. Since this was my third marriage and his second (his first wife died after 51 years of marriage), we decided to keep it plain and simple. The only people in attendance were our witnesses and the mayor of the town, who performed the ceremony. Jacki and Steve from the Texas Wolf Song and Jack, a Coast Guard Academy classmate of Don's, along with his wife, Sharyn, were our witnesses.

We all stayed at a Bed-and-Breakfast (B&B) that in the past had been a private home owned by one of Don's ancestors. We were married in the side garden by a spring. It had snowed during the night. By morning, eight inches of very wet spring snow covered the ground and clumped on the huge pine trees that stood guard in the garden. We hesitated about performing the ceremony outside in these conditions, but the mayor said he was game. The owners of the B&B quickly shoveled the sidewalk and off we went. Since it was cold, coats were needed. It didn't matter what was underneath, so we all decided to keep on the clothes we were wearing. My "wedding attire" became an old jean skirt I had worn the day before. A poem written by Twylah became an appropriate marriage pledge to each other.

Umbrellas and plastic rain hats kept the clumps of snow falling off the pine trees from falling on our heads. On the way to the restaurant to celebrate our union, we had to drive over one of those famous Pennsylvania mountain ridges. The road had not been plowed yet and a car slid off the side blocking all from passing. We had to wait for equipment to reach the scene and clear the road before we could proceed. All in all, our wedding day turned out to be quite an adventure and one we will never forget. After the wedding luncheon, we traveled to Baltimore for a Coast Guard Academy Reunion Dinner.

The girls and I had been on our own for over six years. Having a stepfather in the house was a major adjustment for them. Don was a retired military officer whom they would not be able to finesse as they did their father. At the time, they seemed okay with the wedding arrangements, but later I learned Mel had felt left out. She bemoaned, "Why couldn't we have been there? Dad included us in his wedding." I explained this was my third time getting married; I didn't want to make a big deal out of it. The marriage was squeezed into the Baltimore dinner weekend. It was just a civil ceremony performed by the mayor. Mel confessed, "Well, it was a big deal to me. I wanted to be there!" I had thought of including the girls, but couldn't figure out the logistics of it all. Unfortunately, I had not realized the impact of not including them. It is one of those things that if I had to do over, I would do differently.

Even with a small Mooney airplane, it's a far reach from the northern neck of Virginia to the southern shore of Lake Erie. After our wedding, Don would spend time with me in Harrisburg during the week and fly back to Virginia on weekends to prepare his house for sale. He had lived in it for over 30 years, so there was a lot of sorting and packing to do.

It was a joint decision that we would not fully co-habit until Melanie graduated from high school in June. By that time, we thought his house would be sold and we would have found a home in the Harrisburg area where I was to finish out my career with the state. A previously scheduled Coast Guard Reunion Alaskan Cruise would serve as our delayed honeymoon. Although this set-up is not the normal chain of events for a newly married couple, it was all right with us as there were family responsibilities to take into consideration.

Nor was it the normal chain of events for a senior about to graduate. Mel's senior prom was probably one of the most happy events in her short life. She had a steady boyfriend, *she* chose her prom dress this time, and her uncle chauffeured them in his dark burgundy limousine. She looked stunning in her purple gown. A month before, I was passing through a store when a gown caught my eye. I said to Le'Anne, "Melanie would look great in this dress."

As the prom approached, Mel went shopping with her friends to choose their special dresses. Upon returning she asked, "Mom, will you go to the store with me to see the dress I picked out? I'd like your opinion before I buy it." When I saw the dress I exclaimed, "Melanie, this is the exact same dress I told Le you would look great in!" A mother knows.

Don was staying a weekend with us in Erie. During the night, Mel called out to me from her bed. She started for my bedroom, but collapsed in the hallway. Although her breathing seemed regular, she was not responsive. There was no light in her eyes, only a blank expression. After waiting what seemed like several minutes to see if she would recover, an ambulance was called. At the hospital I was told her blood pressure had bottomed out and a cardiologist was to be called. She was scared.

It was just a short time before when she came home from school and said, "Becky asked me why my speech is slow. I don't think I talk slow, do you?" I did notice a change in her handwriting. I knew these were all signs of Ataxia bearing down on her. We had been through many bouts of her father passing out, taken to the hospital only to have the doctors finding nothing wrong. It was to be many years before he received a correct diagnosis. Mel bared witness to the changes in her sister and father and wanted desperately to deny this was to be her future also.

She was kept in the hospital for over a week as they took tests and tried several medications that didn't seem to help. She kept fainting, she couldn't stand, she couldn't sit up on the side of her bed, she was quite weak, and she was not eating. "I hate this hospital food, I can't stomach it. Bring me McDonalds!" she commanded.

It was the day before graduation, and the doctor wouldn't release her to attend. Mel was to miss an important passage in her life. As to be expected, she was quite despondent. "If he won't release me, I'm just going to walk out!" she declared. Upon standing, she would get dizzy and fall to the bed. "It's the medicine that's doing this. Why do I have to take this medicine? It's not helping. Just let me go home. I want to go home!"

We tried to make the best of the situation and held our own graduation ceremony in the hospital. Her room was decorated and her cap and gown hung where she could see them from her bed. The nurses popped in and out to share in the celebration. We each had our picture taken with her as she lay in disappointment. She was anticipating a call from her friends describing the event. She was sure the phone would ring any moment. Finally, she concluded that they must be too busy celebrating. If only they knew how much she needed their friendship that night.

Due to scheduling conflicts with her friends' graduation parties, Mel's couldn't be held until July. By then we were in the process of moving. Our house was torn apart, boxes were piled everywhere. The party was to be held 60 miles away at my sister's house. Mel bemoaned, "Why can't we have it at our house? It's too far away for my friends to attend." All the family attended. Her friends did not. She was disappointed.

Le'Anne was excited to be moving, Mel was not. She didn't like moving away from her friends. I explained that their tight knit circle would be changing as each set off in different directions to attend college in the fall. Mel tried gaining entry into a small college outside of Erie, but her grades and extracurricular activities didn't warrant acceptance. She settled for a community college in Harrisburg, but her heart wasn't in it. She went because it was expected of her. At the end of the year, they requested that she not return. Although I knew education was the key to a better life, Mel didn't seem to care. When she was in high school, her brothers would often tease her about her poor grades, saying if she didn't bring them up, she would wind up working in the local discount department store. Their prediction came true.

Chapter 16

It is now the year 2000. Although I've talked with Twylah on the phone, I haven't had the opportunity to be in her physical presence since her 85th birthday in 1997. Wolf Song XI is to take place this year. When we found out Gram was attending, both Susan and I set aside money so we could be with our beloved Twylah once more. Although the opening ceremony was to take place on Saturday morning, Bob asked if we could arrive on Thursday so we could assist him with last minute details as his wife was unable to attend.

Flying out of different cities in Pennsylvania, Susan and I met at the airport in Charlotte, N.C. A rental car took us the rest of the way. It was a far drive from the Charlotte airport to the rugged blue-misted landscape of the western highlands. We laughed and joked about the too numerous to count roadside antique stores whose merchandise looked as old and weathered as the rest of the landscape. Susan declared, "Antiquing must be the major industry in this section of the state!" It looked more like junk to me—junk that had been sitting outside for eons.

It was growing dark as we started our winding ascent up the narrow mountain road that lead to the retreat at the summit of Little Scaly Mountain. After stopping to eat at the only restaurant we had seen in hours, we finally arrived in pitch blackness to the silent stillness of the mountain.

Finding the path to the registration office turned out literally to be our first stumbling block. It was so dark. There was only a small light in the distance to point out the way. We couldn't see where we were walking and stumbled several times. The second stumbling block was finding a note saying to register in the morning. What to do? At this late hour, we just wanted to lay our heads down on a soft pillow. The only other building showing light was a short walk away. Again, we set out in the darkness and again we stumbled.

We entered the main lodge via a great room. Off this room was a hall that led to the guest rooms. We surmised these rooms were probably reserved for the Elders, but it seemed nobody had arrived yet. So we did what any other person would do at this late hour...we picked a room and hopped into bed!

In the morning, we awoke to a beautiful view. It appeared we were on the tallest peak in the mountain chain. The lodge was built into the side of the terrain affording mountain vista views as far as we could see. The early morning mist gathered in the valleys below made it seems as if we were in Shangri-La. The trees bordering the retreat were dwarfed by the swirling mountain top winds. It seemed we were on top of the world. It was the perfect spot to hold a Peace Elders Council.

Susan and I handled the registration and anything else Bob required of us. We were working day and night making last-minute adjustments to the program and doing whatever else was needed. We also served as helpers to two Elders. Our task was making sure the Elders were comfortable. When our assignments were revealed, I exclaimed, "Oh Susan, how lucky you are to get Grandmother Sara!" I was also lucky to be with Grandmother Miriam. She was so kind and gentle. We had such a good time together. I made her laugh by running alongside the golf cart that took her from building to building as if I couldn't leave her side. It's fun to play Coyote...people tend to think I'm a blonde airhead and then POW...the Scorpio stings! It's a good way to catch my opponents off guard. Twylah always told me, "It's good to have people oppose us. A good enemy keeps us alert and on our toes."

This Wolf Song brought the Council back to the basics that Gram had originally envisioned. No 109 Elders present on this mountaintop...just 13 including Twylah...like the medicine wheel...with Twylah sitting in the center as our vibral core. There were no hay bales to separate the Elders from the guests; the Elders ate in the same dining room and held workshops for the guests. It was a very intimate gathering. The best one I ever attended. Perhaps it was because Twylah was present at this one. She hadn't attended since the inaugural one that took place on her land.

After all the guests left and the Elders were packed and the cars loaded, Bob, Twylah, Susan, and I had a few minutes to conduct a post review before we got on the road for the long trip home. We were mentally, emotionally, and physically exhausted. We had given all to those who came to hear the wisdom of the Elders. Bob had asked if I would assist at the next Wolf

Song. Unfortunately, I had to say, "not now." I had used up all my precious vacation time to assist with this one. My husband and I were to travel abroad the following year and I would have no vacation time to spare. This was the second time I had to say "not now" to their request for help and it pained me immensely. Twylah's teachings were my passion, but so was my family. The timing was not right…not yet.

Many of the "old wolves" fell out of communication with Twylah when she moved to Florida. Perhaps the time had come for me to cut the apron strings. After all, Twylah told me more than once that she had taught me everything she knew. I would call and find the number had been changed; I would write and receive no reply; I would e-mail and hear nothing back. Her family was keeping her well protected from the masses. However, *I know* that she is always with me. She told me so…many times…many ways.

o o o o o

Time passed and I heard there was a gathering to be held in England. Gram, Bob, and his wife stayed with my friend, Janet. Susan went over to help take care of Twy while Bob and his wife traveled across Great Britain sharing the teachings. Oh, how I envied Susan being there. Unfortunately, I didn't have the vacation time to join them.

Susan revealed that the three of them shared many days carrying on a dialogue concerning spiritual growth. Susan filled Gram in on how the three of us feel we have a joint spiritual mission. We know there is a fourth person, but we don't know who it is. It seems a fourth person would come in and join us for a while, leave, and then be replaced by another. We feel we need a definite fixed fourth to go forward. I guess what came next shouldn't have surprised us, but it did. Gram told Susan and Janet, "I'm the fourth person. I'll always sit in the center of your group, even when I pass into spirit. I will always be there to help and guide you."

It would be six years before my communication with Twylah resumed.

Chapter 17

Journal Entry–April 5, 2003

I like to lie in bed in the morning and think my thoughts. Some do it over a cup of coffee, a morning walk, but I enjoy the soft comfort of my bed.

Spring of 2003 showered us with a refreshing calendar of events that were to take bloom in the summer. I was eagerly anticipating my 40th high school reunion. All my girlhood friends would be in attendance. We hadn't seen or talked to each other since a year after graduation when I moved to Erie.

Mel was eagerly anticipating being an attendant in her friend Becky's wedding. Best of all, she was eagerly awaiting the date set for her jaw surgery. Her regular neurologist was at the Hershey Medical Center. There, she had tried a series of Botox injections that were to relax her jaw muscles enough so she could open her mouth wider to eat and speak. Tears would silently run down her face as each time she would receive eight injections in the sides of her face, jaw, throat, and the back of her neck. She was willing to endure the pain if it produced results. Sadly, there wasn't any noticeable improvement from the efforts. She declined any more injections, any more pain. She was in enough pain already.

While attending a meeting of an Ataxia support group near Philadelphia, we met a neurologist from the University of Pennsylvania. He recommended we see an oral surgeon at the University. This doctor suggested surgery to relieve the constant pain caused by the continual tightening of her facial muscles. She was counting on the surgery bringing relief to her locked jaw and the chronic pain in her back and neck.

To give you some indication of how it felt, sit for a moment with your head erect and tilted a little to the right. Open your mouth a bit and try to push your lower jaw down onto your chest. Stay that way for about thirty seconds. Do you feel the muscles pulling in your throat, your neck, and your upper back? Is your jaw aching? Now try to imagine this kind of pain over a period of years, never subsiding, making it difficult to sleep, to eat, to talk, and to interact with others. She felt as if she was being robbed of her future, her dreams.

It was becoming more and more laborious for Melanie to open her mouth. She could only talk in short bursts; it was getting more challenging for others to understand her speech. Mel started writing her conversations out in long hand. Her nutrition was also suffering. Her meat had to be cut in tiny baby portions. She choked on everything—water, mashed potatoes, meatballs; it didn't matter the texture. She even choked on her own salvia. The choking and swallowing spasms were getting more frequent. No matter how much food she consumed, Mel couldn't gain weight.

Ataxia was always a thorny issue with her. She couldn't accept what the future would bring. She didn't want to end up like her sister. The sister she always made fun of by calling her very biting, hurtful, nasty names; the sister who was paving the trail and marking the signposts that Mel would surely follow. Only this trail was not the fertile garden path of life, it was its antithesis.

Like weeds in a garden, the jaw surgery pushed everything else that was planned aside, killing my reunion and almost choking out her walk down the aisle as a bridesmaid. Unfortunately, like the deadliest weed killer, the surgery almost wiped her out of existence.

We were following the yellow brick road to Philadelphia, to the wizard of an oral surgeon who would hopefully grant a portion of her wish of having a normal life like everyone else. Mel, my husband, and I settled into the hotel that adjoined the hospital and sleeplessly awaited the rising of a new dawn. There wasn't much talk; we were occupied in our individual thoughts and prayers. The morning light brought the much anticipated surgery. Melanie went into the operation very optimistic. She beamed, "The next time Jeremy (her fiancé) sees me, I'll look much different." It turned out to be a very prophetic statement.

The oral surgeon and a resident doctor performed the operation. Going in, Mel knew the odds. The surgery could make her jaw better, worse, or not change it at all. She was placing her odds on making it better, on the surgery being the magic elixir for her future. Mel had a steady boyfriend for the past several years. They were planning to be married in 2005.

When the doctor came to talk to us after the surgery, he said, "I wish you could have seen her face under anesthesia—all the muscles were relaxed, her face wasn't distorted, her chin wasn't pulled down towards her chest; she was quite beautiful." He stated that her mouth needed to be immobilized for a period to help in the healing.

Mel moved out of recovery and returned to her regular room where my husband and I were waiting with flowers and balloons in hand. She was only in the room a few minutes when an orderly came to take her for a test. I followed alongside her wheelchair as we made our way down the extremely busy corridor filled with lunch carts, gurneys, and visitors. We had only gone a short distance when Mel said, "I don't feel well, I'm going to faint." The orderly didn't know what to do. Because I had been through this before, I barked, "We have to find a place for her to lie down before she falls out of the wheelchair. We have to get her hips elevated." Her body started convulsing. I ran for a nurse as the orderly rushed Mel back to her room as she convulsed all the way. She was having difficulty breathing and couldn't express what was happening. She was scared. So was I. Her eyes were pleading for me to intervene, to help her. I placed my hand on the middle of her back and projected healing energy to flow into her frightened frame.

I thought she was going to die right then and there. I often wonder if it would have been better if she had. It would have prevented her from suffering so much emotional pain and grief in the coming year. It's very difficult for a mother to watch her child suffer…this wasn't something I could put a band-aid on or kiss it to make it feel better.

X-rays revealed that material from the operation had gone down her throat and traveled into her lungs. Oh my God! That's how her paternal grandfather died. He suffered a fractured hip falling off the roof of his home. While in the hospital he had complained about difficulty breathing, but it was lunchtime and hospital staff was scarce. A few hours later, he suffered a heart attack and died. The autopsy revealed that a piece of tissue had traveled from his hip to his lungs. The thought went through my mind, was this to be Melanie's fate also? I prayed, "Oh God, please don't let it be so."

Mel was taken into surgery for the second time. I placed a call to her boyfriend saying, "Please come right away, things had taken a turn for the worse. Melanie needs you to be by her side, she needs your moral support to get through this." He said, "I'll leave right away."

It was around midnight when Mellie returned from the second surgery in one day. If only the doctors would have been more careful the first time, this emergency surgery would not have been necessary. She was on a respirator to help her breathe, to give her lungs a break. After the initial surgery, the oral surgeon warned us that her jaw must be kept immobile to avoid nerve damage. I thought, "What effect was the insertion of the respirator tube going to have on that nerve?" The doctor must have been thinking the same thing. He was in attendance throughout the night and much of the next day. He appeared as worried as we were.

Finally, Mel's boyfriend arrived. We prepared him on how she would look before allowing him to enter the room. My words must not have adequately described her appearance. He managed to make it to the side of her bed before fainting and hitting the back of his head against the wall, knocking himself out. Don accompanied him to the emergency room while I stayed with Mel.

Two hours had passed since they headed towards the emergency room. Mel was not yet awake, and I hadn't heard from the men. Could Jeremy be worse then we initially thought? Should his parents be contacted? I decided to go to the ER. When I finally located them, Jeremy was receiving his release instructions. It turned out he had low blood sugar from not eating.

It was now around three in the morning. Instead of going back to Mel's room we decided to go to the hotel and get some sleep as it had been a long 21 hours. After receiving anesthetic for the second time in one day, I thought she would sleep through the rest of the night. I was wrong. When she woke up and found nobody present in her room, she told me, "I thought I had died." Unbeknownst to us all, this episode was to commence the last year of her life.

Her friend's wedding was to take place in one month. A month is not enough time to recover from two surgeries. Melanie was unable to talk, to move her mouth. The surgery wasn't successful. Nothing changed for the better. Her face was still distorted and now the nerve in her jaw was damaged. She couldn't feel the drool dripping out of the corner of her mouth. There was no feeling on the left side of her face. She said, "It feels as if I have a permanent shot of Novocain that's just starting to wear off." The oral surgeon said the nerve may or may not rejuvenate. Time would tell.

Melanie so loved her friend that she didn't want to disappoint her, to short change the wedding party by not being able to attend. I don't know how she managed, but she walked down the aisle in her pale lavender bridesmaid dress. It was to be the last walk down the aisle she would ever take.

o o o o o

Once again, the Earth was cycling into fall and all was not well in the relationship with her fiancé. A mother can see the signs. Their Christmas was not as joyful as it had been in the past. By the end of January 2004, the engagement was off. They never talked to each other again. She was devastated. As is her nature, she didn't want to talk about it. She would just say, "It's over." In the ensuing weeks, she offered few details of what had occurred to bring their engagement to an end. It was becoming increasingly difficult to understand her speech; I had to listen with intense concentration as she repeated a sentence several times in order to catch what she was trying to say. Talking hurt her jaw. Finally, I would ask her to write it down. She would just give up and walk away...as she did with life a few months later.

She was depressed. Her whole life had been devoted to being with him. Now she had nothing to look forward to, nothing to fall back on. She was no longer able to work and had recently applied for social security benefits.

One evening, upon seeing her forlorn form hunkered over the computer, I once again offered, "Mel, would you like to talk to a counselor about your feelings? This would be a neutral party, not a biased mother who though he wasn't right for you anyhow." She came back with, "No, I don't need a counselor." She said *NO* to any suggestions to help jump start her life.

She needed a break from the recent disappointments life had hurled her way. Where could she go? My family was tied up with dramas of their own. I asked her father's side if she could stay with one of them for a while thinking they could help apply salve to her wounds, give her time away to heal the scars, and to map out a fresh start; perhaps, try school again. At the time, nobody in the family could accommodate her. She felt horribly rejected, alone. Tensions in the house and at work were mounting.

With the retirement of our bureau director, three bureaus merged into one. Our new director venomously disliked the old administration and our recently retired director in particular. You see, she outfoxed him in many ways and showed he was an inept political appointment. It's my opinion that because I was closely linked to her (she was my boss when we were in Erie), he disliked me also. Oh hell, he disliked all of us in the other two bureaus! He wanted to be rid of us all so he could build his own fiefdom.

About five years before this merging of bureaus, I had attended a spring conference in Hershey. At the conference, a new federal initiative on one-stop services for employment/re-employment/training was unveiled. I came back to Erie with some casual observations for my boss, Linda. I thought the person, along with the bureau director handling the new initiative for our state were in way over their heads. I said if she ever thought of furthering her career by going to Harrisburg, now was the time; they needed her organization skills. Did my words plant a seed? That fall she went to Harrisburg and started a new bureau to implement the federal initiative. I followed shortly on a special assignment with my bureau. After the federal initiative was up and running, Linda received a promotion and became director of my bureau, her old one. I became her executive assistant. Upon her retirement, the director she had outfoxed assumed control.

The increasing stress in my life was escalating due to the reorganization at work and at home with Melanie's situation. Adding to this, I was also responsible for my other daughter and young granddaughter. This took a physical toll on me.

In 2001, Le'Anne had a baby girl. When Morgen was one-week old, Le'Anne decided to leave the father and move back home. This arrangement didn't work. Le and Melanie fell back into their old routine of fighting all the time, like they did in their childhood. Le decided to strike out on her own and rent an apartment. Although it gave her a sense of independence, it turned out to be more work for Don and myself. Le couldn't drive and wouldn't take a bus. At eighteen months, Morgen started attending the daycare center where I worked. Each morning I would pick her up and drop her off each night.

I don't know what Le did during the day, but she sure wasn't cleaning her house. One day after work I received a body massage and then went to Le'Anne's to clean. While there, I became very weak and tired, so I went home and went straight to bed at 8 PM. I still wasn't feeling well the next morning but went to work anyway. It was lunchtime before I called the doctor and was instructed to immediately go to the emergency room. Finding nothing wrong, I was sent home. After a series of odd disturbances in my cognitive abilities, my husband said we are going back to the emergency room. I spent several days in the hospital going through Cat Scans and MRIs only to be told I have a rare form of migraine headache that affects cognitive abilities. They said the migraines would increase in frequency. Whatever the cause, I've yet to have another episode. So much for the diagnosis of recurring migraines. Perhaps, it was just plain stress seeking relief.

o o o o o

One lazy Saturday in April as I sat watching TV, Mel came into the room asking, "Mom, what are your thoughts on reincarnation?" This was something new for Mel, as she never embraced my spiritual beliefs. She continued with, "I think we live more than one life. Do you?" I replied that perhaps we don't live other physical lives, that perhaps memories of other lifetimes may be carried in our DNA. That perhaps they are memories of our ancestors. I just don't know. She said, "Well, I do believe in reincarnation, I believe we lived before and will live again."

Chapter 18

The warm winds of May were at play as my husband and I prepared for our trip to the Alsace region of France. I was looking forward to finding the birthplace of my paternal grandmother. The plans were in place a year ago when Mel's time was taken up with her fiancé and she had no income. Now she was a "free agent" receiving social security benefits.

It has been a year since the operation. After years of Mel wearing braces, they are now gone. She possesses the wide smile of a Cheshire cat. Drool is still dripping from her mouth, and there are no signs of nerve rejuvenation. As we pack for the trip, we tease her saying, "Too bad arrangements can't be made at this late date for you to join us. Maybe we could put you in a cat carriage and take you with us. We could tuck you under our seat and drop morsels of food into the cage." She enjoyed being teased. She loved humor. She craved attention, any attention.

While we were away, she was to visit her brother Wayne and his family in Edinboro. His son, Markus, was her godchild. She loved him to pieces. Upon our return she related, "Guess what? Markus gave me a hug and kiss goodbye." It was the first time he went to her without crying. He's a shy, reserved child who finds it hard to warm-up to people he doesn't see all the time. She left for Edinboro two days before our departure for Paris. We later learned she came home the day we left. Why? She was suppose to stay longer. This is one of the many questions left unanswered.

We arrived home on Wednesday, June 16. She seemed more remote, more withdrawn than before. She didn't ask about our trip and could have cared less about hearing the details. I'm not even sure she was happy to see us.

o o o o o

While we were gone, it seems Melanie found some new companionship in the form of two males named Andrew and Justin.

The following events ignited the long fuse of explosive emotions that surrounded the tumultuous last week of Melanie's life. I'd like to take you through it day-by-day so you can try to grasp her spontaneous resolution. There is no sugar coating of the facts, only the truth, for it is in the truth that we come to terms with our regrets, our sorrow, and our grief.

Thursday–June 24

In an e-mail to Andrew, Melanie wrote:

Diamond in the back. Yeah, real slick. Leavin me at the red light then speeding off. I had no idea where you went. Justin called my house and gave me a number to call you at. So I did. Whoever answered said you were in the back or something getting catfish bait and he'd have you call me when you got out in like 10-15 minutes. Well, that was an hour and a half ago. All I'm sayin is if nothing else, you need to thank me for that money. Saving your ass is what that is. An apology would be nice too.

Oh, you wanna know what I want for my birthday? Well, my birthday is March 20th. I bought my car around then, like April 1st. For my birthday, all I care about is friends, family, my car, dolphins, animals, and myself. (You fall into the friends' category.) Ya know, when I want something, I go out and buy it. So I never know what to tell people. Usually I get money and bath and body stuff. What I really want to do is go to Sea World and Disney World again.

Ever live with a rich Italian family? Awesome! By the way, if you know anyone who needs to buy an engagement ring, I still have mine ½ karat diamond, 14 karat gold, cost $1000. I paid for it cuz he kept about over $1000 worth of my stuff and the money I lent him.

And I have no idea when I'm going to York to see Jess and get Nick outta the hole and pick-up my letter from him. Nick's getting on my nerves.

Campin this weekend, let's roll. I'm down. You just gotta hit me up with the info, you can call anytime day or night cuz I'm an insomniac. I take Unisom and just listen to Alicia Keys or Ashanti till I fall asleep. Shit, I'm losin days, it's Thursday AM

Yeah, Bacardi Silver is good, triple X. I don't drink much. Only been really drunk once, where everything was spinnin and I had rubber legs. (I didn't feel like pacing myself. So after 3 mudslides I chugged two glasses of Yuengling.) A friend drove me home.

But we all (meaning my ex and his buds) used to go camping at this one site and bumped music and rode four wheelers. First time I pissed in the woods. But I had to work like at 11 AM I had a work ethic so we slept in his truck and left right away.

I never slept in a tent, unless you wanna count the time me, Becky and Ashlee slept in her tent in her backyard.

Yeah, I've been involved in accidents before. One time I sprained my ankle and it swelled up like a balloon and I was on crutches for like a month. I hit 2 deer in my Saturn, $5000 for repairs. Crappy plastic cars. Dent resistant my ass. I've gotten 3 warnings for speeding and a cop clocked me doing 75 in a 50 but I told him I was lost and he just gave me a $90 fine for reckless driving. So, no points... score.

Friday Evening–June 25

Mel hit two mailboxes on Linglestown Road. She arrived home to find that Don and I had gone to bed early. She left a note saying she turned around to look in the back seat to see if her purse was there and lost control of the car.

In an e-mail to Justin, she asked:

What am I going to tell my step dad? I mean, I don't think he'll be mad, it's my car. But I'm under his insurance. It's like military insurance. Oh God, oh God, oh God, what the heck am I gonna say? I can't just say, oh, I was doing 50 in a 35, and turned the light on, and was looking in the back for my purse and accidentally drove up on somebody's lawn and hit 2 mailboxes. God, what if they find me? Am I gonna go to jail? I mean, that car is my baby, my pride and joy, how could I be so careless? I mean, I know accidents happen, but I should have been watching the road. What was I thinking looking behind my seat while driving? Am I stupid? Oh, hurry up and get on, cuz I have no idea what to say. I wanted to go fishing or camping tomorrow, or clubbing, but now I have no car. I'm too sad to even swear in Italian.

Saturday–June 26

In the morning, we found her note and checked out the car. It had damage. She had just bought it six weeks ago. A stripe was added to each side just last week. We got her out of bed and traveled along the road, trying to find the spot of the accident. The mailbox she demolished belonged to an older woman who reported it to the Lower Paxton Police. The neighbor's mailbox was on an iron pipe; this was the cause of most of the damage to the car. We gave the woman our insurance information and then went home to call the police. All we got was a message saying if it's an emergency, call another number. Since we didn't think it an emergency, we told Mel we would report it on Monday. Don called the insurance company and arranged for the repairs. He helped her drop off the car at the designated dealer.

Neither Don nor I were upset about the accident. We handled it very calmly, matter of fact, never raised our voices. The insurance would take care of it. We were just glad nobody was injured.

We assumed she was going over the speed limit. Mel always drove too fast for her slow responses. Upon receiving her driver's license, the test instructor warned her about going too fast. I was always pushing the imaginary brake pedal when riding with her. This has been Mel's third accident since moving to Harrisburg. We speculated that our insurance would go up with this one!

In an e-mail to Justin, she wrote:
> *Well, we went down there this morning. I uprooted the lady's mailbox and her neighbor guy's that was on an iron post. The lady was home and she was old and was just glad noone was hurt. The guy wasn't home but she said he tried fixing it last night but cut his hand. He put the mailbox back this morning but was not at home when we were there. I hope he didn't go to the ER. Anyhow, my stepdad's on the phone with my insurance right now. I'm just ashamed.*

In an e-mail to Andrew, she wrote:
> *Well, I found out what I hit. I uprooted the one mailbox which was wooden I guess, and then I smashed the fender with the iron bar. I don't wanna talk about it. I can't believe I messed up.*

In the evening, Don and I met some friends for dinner. We got home around 11:30 PM to find all the lights in the house on, both the computer and the lights in the basement were on; a package of hot dogs lay open on the kitchen counter, and a skillet stood on the stove. It was as if she had just left the room and would return.

This is the just the type of irresponsible behavior that irks us. Why couldn't she take the time to put the meat away and turn off all the lights? Why the big rush? We were always harping on Melanie about not cleaning up after herself. Letting meat sit out to spoil was going a bit far. We would have to talk to her about this.

Then we found a note stating she went to Ocean City, Maryland, with her friend Jessica and her family (this was a lie) and that she would return on Tuesday. Why didn't she call my cell phone instead of leaving a note? She left a number where she could be reached. Upon her return, she destroyed the number. I had never met this Jessica and don't know when they became friends.

Sunday–June 27th

Upon looking at the calendar for the coming week, I noticed Mel had a dentist appointment on Monday and a neurologist appointment in Philadelphia on Tuesday. These were important appointments.

I called the number she left and thought it funny that I didn't get a voice greeting, only a beep. I left a message asking Melanie to call me. She did. It was a terse brief call. I gave her the phone numbers of the doctors and stated SHE would have to cancel the appointments or pay for them; I was not going to do it for her. She said she would. She didn't.

Monday–June 28th

Don got two calls from the credit union asking how they could get in touch with Melanie; they were questioning her unusual withdrawal of money. Don called Melanie and in the brief call, she stated that she was taking care of it. He didn't understand how she knew.

Tuesday–June 29th

We were in our bedroom when Melanie arrived home about midnight. I said we would talk to her tomorrow; it was too late to get into a discussion tonight. I wanted some sleep.

Wednesday–June 30th

Don called me at work and said he and Melanie had a heated discussion. He stated, "I chewed her out good over her lack of responsibility." I inquired, "How did she respond?" He replied, "She just sat and listened."

He said it was all right between the two of them now. I called Melanie and she said nothing about their discussion, so I didn't either. I figured Don had already covered our complaints, so there was no reason for me to rehash it; she had gotten the point.

Don was going to be away overnight, so I asked what she wanted me to bring home for dinner. While eating, I asked how her weekend went, and she just gave a quick reply. It's hard to carry on a conversation because of her difficulty in speaking, so I left it at that.

However, she did say something that struck me as strange. She asked, "Mom is it all right if I go to Ocean City again over the July 4th holiday?" It was the tone of her voice, a resignation as if her heart wasn't in it, as if she wanted me to say no. Last Saturday, she just went with no discussion. Apparently, she did get the point.

She revealed, "We met some men there and one has a father who lives nearby." She continued, "Justin is already there with his father. Andrew and I are going to drive down after my appointment in Philadelphia." I asked, "Mel, do you feel comfortable being with three men you hardly know?" She feebly responded, "I have no problem with this." I had some hesitation about her going, but since she is 23 years old I didn't think I had much say in it. I made a mental note that I had a few more days to discuss it with her and went to bed early.

In an e-mail to Justin, she wrote:

> *You were in the tent sleeping right, and Andrew was in his truck sleeping, and since Lori had to wake me up at 7:30 AM to look for her shampoo (for God's sake, it's a $1 bottle of shampoo). I took the liberty of changing into my bikini in front of you. So, yeah, I got*

2 hours of sleep and when we first got there, you two napped, but I couldn't becuz Andrew kept looking at me and yelling at me in his sleep, so I went swimming in the lagoon and took a walk along the pier and got a soda, came back and got on the mattress with you. I got to sleep probably about 5 minutes, and then Andrew woke me up again with his sleep talking. I woke up with a huge headache so I took some Advil, came back in, you were awake and I couldn't fall back to sleep. Yo, I don't know who kept sayin, "I'm the one out of us 3 who has gotten the least sleep, so leave me alone." That ground was so uncomfortable though. Why did you make me sleep on the ground? That mattress is plenty big enough for the 2 of us.

Oh, my brother used to drive a Jetta, now his wife does and he drives his Explorer. But I loved to do the key. Just how it likes pops up. Hmm, you 2 have got to stop walking ahead of me. Hmm, that first night I told him to stop, he's like, Not now, I'm talking to Justin." So I fell behind, eventually took the shoes off, some guy comes up to me like, "Can I buy you a drink?" I'm like,"Oh thanx, but no thanx." Then I walked past a group of wolf whistling guys. Then I walked by another group of guys, a guy said hi. I walked past this girl and her b/f and their friend IK guess, black afro guy. He's like, "I lost my baseball, can you help me find it?" Then I think you saw how I walked past those guys, the one did a twirl into me and is like, "Oh, I'm sorry, you can come back." And that one night you 2 guys went off with the cop, some Asian kids our age were out on the patio of their hotel restaurant. He's like, "Hi, you hungry I'll buy you anything." Ha, Ha, then that guy you two waved at. Cuz I'm sayin I kept lookin back, I couldn't see a face, just to be like "Bitch, don't be lookin at my boys." And he's like "Hi!

And who told you Andrew and I have known each other a month. He saw me in a chatroom once and sent me his picture. I IM'ed him and said, "Yeah, showin me how cute you are dude?" Then he told me to call him, like right away. I told him why? I wouldn't so he's like, "My best friend just asked me to go camping, wanna come?" I'm like "No, another time." So, that next night we met at Sheetz, then the next night I think I paid his ticket, then the next night, your car, then the next night, Ocean City baby, yeah. Short month. Ha, Ha!

I've got all of my dolphin stuff just staring at me. I can't remem-

ber if my eyebrow ring was $48 or $68, my tattoo was $250. Yeah, it was really kewl how Andrew always came in the tent to talk to me. Oh, that was you! ☺ Andrew likes you more than me.

And Andrew should be glad I didn't get a ticket. That truck is registered to one Nancy ----. I'm just like "um, yeah." I have no idea who that is. So, it woulda gone on his record. This is the 4ᵗʰ warning I got. Then he's like "Yeah, sweetie, I didn't tell you that this handles differently cuz it's AWD. I'm thinking, "So is my Subaru, but I'll let him win this one!"

All I ate today was 6 chicken McNuggets. I just didn't think about hunger. Too busy thinking about dolphins and what's up with Andrew. He hasn't even kissed me yet. I mean, I told him I'm real touchy and don't usually like to be touched. But you saw me wrap my arms around him, It's like "DUDE, TAKE A HINT!" I need a picture for my frame. Well than, off we are, time for bed. Cheerio darling.

A second e-mail to Justin:

If your girl is coming on this trip with us for the 4ᵗʰ of July, I'd be afraid something would happen.

A third e-mail to Justin:

Did you call my bank? Cuz you have the receipts and stuff. I gotta call my dentist; I was supposed to go there Monday. Then I was supposed to go to my neurologist on Tuesday, which is why my mom got so bent up. Then she's like, Jessica Smith, r u sure? That sounds like a fake name. Ya know what, I don't care if you wound up dead." And she just hung up. I thought it was funny but you 2 were all worried. Then my stepdad called cuz of the bank. I'm like, "Damm guys, stop worrying, I'm 23, I'm not gonna get sent home." My stepdad didn't ask me about my trip and my mom just called from work to pick-up supper, she won't ask. They just like to scare me. But they don't. God damn lesbians wakin me up and shit, and this morning my stepdad woke me up. He's like, "Tomorrow I'll let you sleep, OK sweety?"

You can meet my parents. My other screen name is zingofthe-day1. I never use it but there's a picture of me and my mom on it. She's nice, but she is a bitch, but she'll be nice to you. And my *stepdad's fun. My ex-finance and him got along real well. Ew, in a year I coulda been married, brr. If we all go to the beach again, it'd be safer if they knew you. And damn, I wanna do that again. $300 is really like nothing compared to the fun we all had. And I can drive; we can race although my car is 4 cylinders automatic it's still zippy. If you beat me, you can eat me. Hahaha. Hmm, I've been to Myrtle Beach twice, Florida Beach a bunch of times and I grew up in Erie, with Lake Erie. So I always went to the beach. But the only place I have gone without family is with my ex-boyfriend and his band. We all drove to Philly, oh, and Toronto, they had a gig in Toronto. But that wasn't really fun. I hate death metal, that's what they play. How's your toe? Something bit you, were you just lying to get the lesbians to suck it while you f----- em in the ass. I know that sounds raunchy but they are ugly ass scheming tricks. And they told me to keep those pants. I'm throwin em out, they have like holes and stains and icky gunk. Um, Mom's home, later skater*

In an e-mail to Andrew, she wrote:

Thank you for the gifts, I love em. I actually have a big collection of snow globes in my bedroom, but none of dolphins, now I have 2. They had lots of dolphin things at the place I went to, but I didn't buy em cuz I had to buy a towel and a bikini, and I wasn't sure how much money I had in checking. That card comes directly from my checking account, see, I keep the bulk of it in savings.

Anyway, I had a bad feeling about those lesbians, Nicole and Lori. I mean, they were uncommonly very nice to us all of a sudden after dude left. They didn't even come over and say hi to us when we first got there. Then when we went to the store that second time, Nicole is like thank you. I'm like for what? I don't have any money. She's like, "What? He told me you would pay." So what the crap was I gonna do? Yeah, she kept telling me she'd pay me back. Um, I don't think so when they couldn't even afford to buy their own food. But Lori came in the tent at 7:30 this morning and tried waking Justin up but couldn't, then she woke me up like "Where's my shampoo?" Honestly, I musta dropped it, but it was like a 90-cent bottle of shampoo. She got so bent outta shape, then I didn't wanna wake either of you up so I went over to Lori's.

Nicole was still sleeping I had Kool-Aid and stuff, and then went to the tent to get on my bikini (which bikinis are not for swimming.) Then went back to give her towel and stuff, then Nicole's like, "Lori, tell her I wanna talk to her." I was right there. She's like, "You know how we have to leave today. Well, can you put 2 more nights on your card for us?" I'm like, "Ahh, I really can't." She's like, "OK, think about it."

So I went back to the tent and told Justin (I know how you hate when I wake you up.) I told him and he's like, "Go get Andrew and tell him we gotta roll." Which I couldn't even do, why can't I sleep like that? Then when we were packing up the tent, yes, I helped, you gave me a hard time about swimming instead of helping, but it's OK.

Anyway, Nicole's like, "Lori, where's our shampoo?" She said she didn't know. "Well, did you look in her bag?" "No, she said it's not in there." "Well, look anyway." That's when I ran and got my purse and started freaking out. Then they're like, "I wanna keep in touch, please." I'm thinking, "Yeah, I'm sure we'll never see your asses again and frankly I couldn't care less."

Do you care? Well, if you do, I can't be there or else I just won't even bring my card to the ocean, but then what would we all do? And they're all asking you guys what you do. You're all like, "We make a good living building."

Hun, they're moochers. I would advise you 2 to never contact them. Please, that whole situation is screwed up and I sensed that from the very beginning. The only reason Nicole kicked dude out was because she saw us and thought, "They look like suckers, we can get the two guys by being lesbians and we'll just tell the girl we love her and be nice to her so the guys will know we're kewl." 2 scheming bitches, that's all. Homeless women.

Anyhow, I had tons of fun on this trip and wanna do it again like real soon. That's what happens when you grow up in Erie. You kinda need to know how to swim. Plus, pool class freshman year, and my uncle has an inground pool, but I haven't been in it like 5 years. But we would be in it every hot summer day. Anyway, you're welcome, cuz you don't have to pay me back all the money. I just was there to have fun and I wanted you to have fun too.

A second e-mail to Andrew:

Jess just said, "F U Mel and leave me alone." Everyone has basi-

cally turned on me today I guess. But I don't even care. My stepdad yelled at me just for stupid shit, nothing I can't handle. The other day he told me I was like a daughter to him and he's always saying how I'm a gem and so great to have around. Now he's being nice to me, so I don't really even know. Stuff like this doesn't really affect me or I'd be insane by now.

Well, I gotta get a job, like really quick. I could go back to the store. I spent a year and a half there, so they love me. I was the hardest worker. Jess is just mad cuz she introduced me to Nick, the guy that was in jail, but I told him I'm seeing you now and he got mad. Oh, he got out like the day of my accident. Yeah, I'm choosing you over him.

A third e-mail to Andrew:

I'm gonna get my car back. They have to order the parts, so until the parts come in, my car would just be sitting there. So my stepdad's gonna take me down tomorrow.

I don't have your # or even know your last name. Mine's Rosthauser by the way. Melanie Jean Rosthauser.

My mom's name is now Jean Vaughn. She has been married 3 times, had 2 sons with the first, he beat her though so she married my dad and had 2 girls. Now my dad lives in Erie. I hardly ever talk to him, he doesn't like me. My stepdad is 81 but doesn't seem it. He was a pilot in WW2 and still is a pilot. I have 4 nieces, Gretchen, Ally, Madison and Morgen, 1 nephew/godson, Markus.

Hmm, I shower at least once a day, if not more. I think you're awesome and I hope you feel the same way about me. I was drunk only once, rubber legs, but I drink so don't worry. I have been high once, I smoked like 6 bowls this one time and nothing. I got high off the bong.

My meds, don't worry, the doctor instructed I take four 10 mg valiums at one time and nothing, that's 40 mgs. Now I take only 5 mg. And 25 mg dantrium but they don't do much; they're for my muscle spasms so my jaw doesn't lock up and hurt. It still does, and not cuz I'm so used to the pills. Since day 1…nothing. My sister-in-law is a nurse and gave a trucker 5 mg of valium and it put him right to sleep

I'm online a lot, actually, I'm always online, just with my away message on, so I can hear you come on.

Thursday–July 1st early morning

In an e-mail to Justin, Melanie wrote:

You know that guy in jail? I told him about this weekend and that I like Andrew, so he lied to Jess and told her I said she was fat and her boyfriend is fat. Which I did not. She kept calling me a little bitch. I am so sick of it. I could so make her suicidal just by saying shit, but I'm not like that. Nick is being so mean just cuz I choose Andrew over him. I can't help it he got sent to jail. When I told Nick he called me a lying slut. Well, not at first. I'm not a slut, do you think I'm a slut ? I've had like 6 partners, if even. And I never lied to him. Yawn, I'm sleepy.

In second e-mail to Justin:

All right, all right, all right. Fire em up. Start the ignition on straight up automobile pimpin. Jess is being mean, yo. She says I'm so shallow. She's bitching at me, I'm just gonna leave again, then I'll have to block her, she harasses me.

In third e-mail to Justin:

My buddy and me. OK, so it's on like cheech and chong and I want some long...OK, OK, I'm stopping. I just gotta get myself out of this bitchy mood.

OK, this time, no Jessica. F her, "F what cha heard cuz my side mirrors flap like a f---ing bird." Actually, right now my right mirror does. It just hangs there and hits my door.

OK, here's what's up. Your mom lives here in Harrisburg so you know Andrew from school. Now, here's where it gets tricky-icky and gooey-ooie. Your dad lives in Ocean City and you visit him. Every July you go and stay with him at his house.

Don't you dare even start to think about anyone calling you. They don't know that's your number and besides, I threw the # out. They're not that diplomatic, they just worry about me. Ya gotta feel me on that one, I know you do huh. Don't freak out. Now, you promised me dolphins, you gonna follow through on this. Like we can go on the fishing boat, you 2 can fish and I can convince the captain to get the dolphins by the boat. Hey, looks and big boobs get you far *in life. So, you'll pick me up tomorrow and drive me to my bank and call that bank in OCMD and tell them that they screwed up, oh know what, there was an 800 number like on the MAC machine, so the bank can call that 800 # and when we get down there, all they'll need is my i.d. then I can walk out with my $400...right?*

And I can pack like sandwiches and chips and pickles and corn and jelly donuts and all kinds of drinks so we won't have to scrounge. Yeah, that's what I'm sayin. And I'll bring shampoo and conditioner and soap and razors and everything. We stayin at the same place. No mooching lesbians this time.

Andrew's like, "You know they're gonna give you a test before you can drive a jet ski right? You got good grades right? Straights F's. Try A's. Yeah...shut up, I grew up in Erie, every girl is rich, pretty, popular and smart. Well, everyone holds their own, that's why I need a jobby job. I'm going back to the store. I guess, bleak, unless I'm gonna look for a good chef job. I did everything at the store. I ran register, took orders, cooked the food, cleaned, just ran around and I hated when I would be the only one there and all of a sudden I get this huge ass line like out the door. People would be yellin at me like, "Miss, can you just make my order cuz I gotta get back to work." I wanted to yell, "Go home lady!" I got so frustrated.

Well, I'm gonna have to pawn my diamond ring out. Hmm, paid $1000 for it, I'd probably get more on ebay. My aunts both sell stuff, and maybe my sister-in-law, I'm not sure.

Yeah, so the 6th through the 12th huh? And this time, I'm gonna bring my cd's. Hey, are you positive, like 100% that Andrew's gonna be all like, "Yeah, I'll pick you up on Tuesday." Wait a minute, OK, he's driving right? So we gotta tell him, or are we just gonna tell him I'm gonna give him the money to go? OK, that sounded pretty half-witted huh? Oh hey, I can't go, but come to my house Tuesday night and I'll float you 300 bux. Yeah...no, I don't think that would work. What are you gonna tell him when you talk to him whenever? (Ew, gag me with a spoon, phlegm is sick and it's like stuck in my throat. This year I've gotten bronchitis 4 times and when I was in college, I had strep throat 3 times.) You should be like, "Yo bro, I can't take ya down but talk to Mel cuz she's got mad dough, and if she goes, you better f--- her. He, he. Oops, you don't have to say he he, but just so we get this shit straightened out with the bank *and my $400.*

Yeah, that place, the campground, the pool hours are 10 AM to 6 PM. Or, like I don't even know if you'll be at your girlfriend's all day. I never carry cash, I always use my card. Controls my spending. I'd rather buy you two cigarettes than 2 homeless ladies. I'm gonna e-mail my dad and tell him I'm getting my car a tune-up and every- thing, and he'll give me $400. I hate being a mooch. But until you cats pay me back, I'm worried, cuz I'm saving for the future so when I get married we don't have to scrounge for money and both work too much, ya know.

I had like $5000, where'd it all go? I put $6000 down on my car. I'll be paying it for 5 years. Andrew wants me to buy a WRX when I trade in my Legacy. Which I was gonna get a WRX, but se- riously, my insurance would sky rocket and why do I really even need turbo. You know, it's actually the same engine, the WRX and my Legacy. I think the WRX is 4 cylinder box engine too, the WRX is just turbo-charged.

K, so are we gonna tell Andrew that we can go on Tuesday? Let me check the calendar real quick. OK, my appointment's at 11 AM Tuesday, so I'll be home at 3 at the latest. I'll tell my stepdad not to stop anywhere cuz he's not a speed demon. Come on, he's 81; he doesn't look it or act it or sound it, so I don't wanna hear another word about my parents. My mother raised me, my dad was there but not really, he didn't pay child support. Plus I'm her baby, don't blame them. I'm gotta tell my mom Andrew is my boyfriend when I get back. OK I just do. She doesn't even know I'm spending my money again. They don't look at my bank statements, I just gotta keep the house clean and I can do pretty much whatever I want, except get arrested for DUI on a hit and run.

This time, I better see dolphins. I'm gonna jump into the ocean and see if I have to make them my family so they'll protect me from sharks. You know, dolphins can kill sharks, even great white sharks. They could kill me. Years ago a dolphin killed a little boy. I forget the rest. I should go back there and find that obnoxious girl on that boat who kept feedin for dolphins and smack her upside the head. Dolphins are mine. Oh, this bruise on my knee, I hit it on my car getting in, I think. And my right knee, its hamburger cuz I got 16 stitches when I was 6 from falling off of my bike, It was so the

*pothole's fault. I was also speeding. I used to race 10 speeds and do
donuts with my pink banana seat bike when I was 5. Crazy!*

*I wanna go back to the Wal-Mart parking lot and just be a
lunatic. Andrew can do donuts in the snow but not dry pavement.
Only I do that cuz it ruins the tires. Any my ex-finance taught me to
drive stick cuz I was always the DD. Then he got an automatic but
I remember pretty much. But his gears were like different, plus yours
has that easy shifter knob with the gears marked. In his truck, neutral was in the center, and like reverse was above 5th. He just had a
plain knob, so it took me awhile, I kept ridin the clutch and stalling
it. I hate stick, but I can do it if I'm forced to, it's just a lot of work.*

*OK, I'm gonna try to stay up and wait for ya, you're picking me
up at 2 tomorrow, so I gotta set my alarm clock. I usually wake up
after an hour, then go back to sleep for another 5. But I have been
losing lots of sleep these past few days. Plus my whole life.*

*I'll wait outside tomorrow or I'll watch for your car. If you
remember where I live even. That's why I'm waitin, I'm about to just
go ahead and call you soon. Nah, it's too late.*

*I don't know why my mom answered that one time. But when I
leave I usually hide my phone, usually put it in my room, they don't
go in there. They probably watch my porn…eww, why did I just say
that? Well, if they do, than they wouldn't ask if I have a boyfriend.
They'd ask if I have a girlfriend. Hahaha! See, I just get worse and
make things worser. R you sure Andrew's vehicle will be fixed by
Tuesday cuz I can't drive on the highways with my mirror hangin K,
I'm goin to lie on the couch and eat.*

In fourth e-mail to Justin:

*You remember how to get to my house? Just take Blue Mountain
Parkway all the way to the stop sign. Turn right onto Parkway East
and then just stay straight onto my road. Address is on the mailbox.
Don't hit it. Just pull in, and don't run over the lights, the UPS
guy kept doing that on the last set we had. Be there at 2 PM, I'll be
waiting, if not, ring the doorbell, no, better yet, if I'm not outside,
call my phone line. If I don't answer that means I went to pick up
my car, and you know how fast I drive. Um, if I don't talk to you
tomorrow you can call me.*

I awoke Thursday morning and decided not to go to work. I wasn't sick, but I was out of sorts. Don's daughter was coming on Friday and the house needed to be cleaned. Sometime in the afternoon, I saw Melanie walking across the yard. She came in through the front door. This was strange because we never use the front door. I asked her if she went for a walk and she replied, "Yeah." I said, "With your purse?" She didn't reply. A while later she asked if she could take my car to Target. I let her. Call it mother's intuition or whatever, I thought she was acting strange and decided to read her e-mails. I didn't like what I saw.

When she came back, I asked if she wanted to open a bank account under my name, a place to hide her savings. I said she could withdraw anytime without my questioning. We had talked about this when she received her payout from Social Security, but I hadn't followed through. She agreed. I asked how much she wanted to put into savings. I recalled that she should have had about $4,000 left.

She retrieved the balance by phone; it was $1,420.85. I had her go into her account history on the phone. I wrote down all her withdrawals. She wrote on paper (because of the difficulty of understanding her speech) that Jessica owes her $300 for a phone bill and she took out $900 today. She wrote that Andrew is paying her back $580 and Justin is to pay her back $320. She said that she trusts them.

For the total month of June, she had withdrawn $3,161.50 from her savings account. From June 23 on, she had withdrawn $2,706.00 of that total amount. She also withdrew $274 from her checking account in various amounts. This totals $2980 in withdrawals in one week!

Up until that time, she usually made withdrawals of $40 or so when she needed money. She was very frugal with her money and prided herself on buying clothes at the end of the season when there were drastic price reductions. At the time of her death, she had $1.55 on her person and $2.30 in her purse.

I was furious. She had gone without money for one-and-one-half years. Why was she giving it away so freely now? I just didn't understand; it didn't make sense to me. I demanded she go online to request the $900 be returned right away, while they still had it. These are the instant messages between Melanie and Justin:

M: *Justin, it's Mel*

J: *why you getting kicked out*

M: *cuz my mom found out*

J: *how did she find out? Some lady called me from your phone skitzing*

M: *so can you bring my $900 to my house now*

J: *well I gave Andrew 400 to hold till he picked you up on tues.*

M: *Justin, bring the money please*

J: *and I gotta get ahold of him and I'm getting ready to leave cant I just bring it up when I get home cause I have amandas whole family waitin for me*

M: *my mom's right here, so*

M: *no*

M: *I'm soo sorry Justin*

J: *tell her the reservations are going to be made at www.coconutmalarie.com*

M: *I typed in: if you do not return the money within 20 minutes the police will be called in*

J: *well your gonna have to call Andrew for the rest of it cause it doesn't have nothing to do with me…*

J: *can your mom meet me on Linglestown road*
There was a long pause as we were discussing the meeting place, how it might not be safe to meet him. Without Justin knowing, I took Melanie's place at the keyboard.

J: *HELLO, Can your mom meet me on Linglestown road?*

M: *I typed in: please hurry or you'll be in trouble*

M: *I typed in: where on Linglestown road*

J: *no can your mom meet me on Linglestown road*

J: *I gotta grab a shower but I don't want no one there but me n her cause i am keeping it real with her and tell her the truth*

M: *I typed in: no shower, NOW*

J: *I'm all dirty but alright meet me at the weis market*

J: *here I'll just bring it up to the driveway and give her Andrew's number okay I'll be right there*

M: *I typed in: Now! Bring the money.*

M: *I typed in: number and money*

M: *I typed in: end of our driveway*

There was a long pause.

M: *I typed in: when are you coming I know you are talking to Andrew*
     (I could see that both were online
M: *I typed in: you can be traced*

Justin became scared when he was told I was calling in the police. He agreed to come to the house to return $500. He stated that Andrew had the rest. While he was on his way to our house, I put in a call to the police. When Justin arrived, I found his conversation very strange. He told us about the trip to Ocean City and how Andrew didn't treat her very well. He wouldn't walk beside her. Justin said, "Andrew went into the car to sleep and left Melanie to sleep on the bare ground. That he, Justin, then let her sleep next to him to keep warm." Justin said his girlfriend went along. If this were true, why would she let Melanie sleep beside him? He said, "Andrew didn't give her any money for food, so I gave her some." How kind, since it was Melanie's money they were spending. He was making himself out to be the good person and Andrew the bad. Since Melanie was supposed to be passing out money freely, why didn't she have any herself? Why didn't she have the receipts from the ATMs? Justin finally gave her the receipts tonight. Justin kept repeating that perhaps we needed to know the truth, as if he were threatening her with something.

I bellowed at Melanie, "These people will be gone when all your money is gone. They are preying on you!" I roared at Justin, "How can you justify taking money from someone who is disabled?" A look of shock appeared on his confused face. He said, "Disabled? I didn't know she was disabled. I thought she just had jaw surgery."

I will never forget the look on Melanie's face. She looked at me with such disgust. To reveal she was disabled was betraying the new persona she was trying to build. With resignation in my voice I said, "Yes, that is true, she had jaw surgery." I didn't reveal that the surgery was a year ago. How foolish I was to say she was disabled. I had learned at work that you do not refer to people as disabled unless they label themselves as such and Mel would never own up to the fact that she had Ataxia.

By that time, the police had arrived. The officer talked to Justin for a while. Justin promised that the money would be returned. Then the police officer came over to me and asked, "Do you want me to talk to her?" I replied, "She might listen to you." He took her aside and warned her not to be so ready to trust people and hand over her money; she should keep it for herself, take a vacation, save for the future. With nothing more to be done, the police officer left. Mel, Justin, Don, and I went inside the house so Justin could write down on paper where all her money had gone. He scribbled:

6/23	200	Andrew speeding ticket
6/25	200	Justin's car
6/26	300	He didn't know
6/27	402	They state the ATM in Ocean City didn't dispense the money even though her account shows the withdrawal.
6/28	302	Justin and Andrew
6/29	302	$100 Justin, $100 Andrew, $100 Mel
6/30	50	He didn't know
7/1	950	Justin and Andrew

The July 1st withdrawals were made from more than one location. Mel didn't have a car. I surmise that Justin must have driven her in the afternoon, hence the purse over the arm when I questioned her as to where she had been.

Justin signed a paper stating he would return $1600 of the money in installments of $500 starting in August. During all this discussion, Melanie was calm; she didn't tell me to butt out of her business nor did she attempt to stop what was taking place. She stood behind me the whole time and leaned over my shoulder to see the amounts Justin was claiming and agreeing to repay.

A strange comment Justin kept making all night was, "I don't want you to think badly of me; after all, I'm going to reimburse all the money I owe. If you meet me in a store or someplace, I don't want you to turn away." This was very much on his mind, that we not think badly of him. If he didn't do anything wrong, why would we think badly of him?

Justin prepared to leave our house around 11 PM. He very emphatically demanded/commanded Melanie go online and get anything in writing she could from Andrew so Justin could then go to a Justice of the Peace to have Andrew reimburse him for Andrew's share of the take. Mel ran past Don to Justin's car window. What she said we do not know.

When she came back into the house, she was frantic to get online with Andrew. We had heated words about her lying about the trip; that she didn't go with Jessica; she was with Justin and Andrew the entire time. I screamed at her, "I can't trust you anymore; this is the last straw. What else are you lying about? You have to leave the house tonight. I don't care where you go, just get out. I can't take anymore." Don added, "Once a liar, always a liar. The thing about liars is that you never know when they are telling the truth, so you can never trust them."

I asked Don to remove her computer from the basement as I proceeded to unhook the one in my office. She tried to stop me. When she realized she wouldn't be able to reach Andrew she became greatly agitated; she actually appeared frightened. She ran out of the room and right into Don as he was carrying her computer to his office in the other garage. She made a low guttural sound at him.

o o o o o

It all happened in a matter of seconds. I heard a horrible gasping sound and immediately after, a second one. I ran into the hall to find her standing at the bottom of the steps leading up from the sunken den into the hallway. She held a bloody knife in her left hand, the Bowie knife she and her ex-finance had given Don as a Christmas present. It laid uncovered on the top shelf of the bookcase by the stairs, the sheathe was to come later. Funny, there was not a lot of blood on it like they show in the movies. Hardly any blood at all.

There was no color in her face, no expression in her eyes. I panicked. I ran up the back steps leading into the garage to get Don. He yelled out, "Call 911!" It was only a matter of seconds until I returned and found her lying on the floor in the hallway with the knife at her feet. I don't know how she managed to make it up the three steps and take several steps down the hallway before collapsing. Those movies again...I remember thinking, "Don't touch the knife."

I picked up the phone, dialed 911 and then sat on the floor beside her. I informed the operator, "My daughter just stabbed herself." In a pleading voice I said, "I'll give you the necessary information when you tell me an ambulance is on the way. Please send an ambulance right away!"

I must remain calm; I knew Mel was able to hear me. If I panicked, she would know it was serious. I didn't want her to be afraid. She was not responding, but she was still breathing. The operator asked, "Is there a lot of blood?" No, there wasn't; in fact, there was hardly any blood at all. I kept staring at the open wound, but no blood was coming out. In looking back, I can't believe I was able to remain so calm. I must have been in shock already.

After what seem like an eternity, the ambulance finally arrived with the police right behind. The police officer took me aside and started asking questions. All I wanted was to see what was happening with my daughter. Was Melanie going to make it? As the police officer was talking to me, he positioned my back towards Melanie as the EMT's moved her from the floor to the lowered gurney. As they were lifting her onto the gurney, she let out a horrible gasp. They carried her up the steps towards the garage.

Don and I quickly secured the house before leaving for the hospital. As we walked into the garage, I thought it strange that Mel was still lying there instead of being rushed to the hospital. I kissed her on the forehead, told her I loved her, and would meet her at the hospital. She was then put into the ambulance. We followed shortly behind.

When we arrived at the Hershey Medical Center Emergency Entrance, there were no parking spaces left. Don dropped me off at the door and said he would meet me inside. As I walked by the ambulance, I noticed two men folding sheets covered with a lot of blood and heard one say to the other, "There goes the mother."

When I walked in and stated my name, I was immediately escorted to an empty room containing a table, a few chairs, and a telephone. I thought this was strange. Why couldn't I see my daughter now? Why did I have to wait by myself in this empty room? What was taking them so long? Finally, Don walked in with the doctor right behind.

The doctor said, "I'm sorry; she didn't make it. We did everything possible. I totally devoted a half-hour to just her case, but she died in transport." In my heart, I knew she had died at home when she gave up that last gasp at life. That last gasp that the police wouldn't let me witness…wouldn't let me be by her side to tell her I loved her as her soul departed her body.

We sat at that barren table that held only a phone, the kind of table a condemned person might sit at waiting for the governor to call with a reprieve. However, no call came. With my husband and doctor looking on, I sat and cried and cried and cried until all the waters of Niagara Falls had drained from my soul. The doctor then asked, "Is there anybody you want to contact?" I knew her grandmother was vacationing in Las Vegas; and I didn't want to call her father with such terrible news without anyone being with him, so I called his brother in Pittsburgh and asked if he could drive up to Erie in the morning.

After making the call, we finally were escorted into the brightly lit cool room where Mel lay dead on the table. As we entered, the attendants moved away from her and stood at one end of the room. The doctor stated, "We have to leave the tube in her mouth until the autopsy. Anytime a death occurs that is not of natural causes there has to be an autopsy."

I looked towards the ceiling because I knew her spirit was still around, that she could still hear my words, still see me. I caressed the side of her face with my hand in the same manner she had done to my mine all those years ago when she had that high fever. I took her hand in mine and started saying my good-byes...for now. Don said the room was dead silent, that everyone present was intently listening to my words; they seemed enthralled with what I was saying. I really don't remember what I said because they were words from my heart. Words from a mother to her daughter, offering unconditional love, saying it was all right, I forgive her, I understand.

With nothing, absolutely nothing left inside me, no tears, no anger, no pain, just shell shocked with the knowledge that my youngest child was no more, we found our way back home, not to sleep, but to try to digest the surrealness of the situation. I found a pail and some rags to clean up the small amount of blood that fell on the steps, leaving a trail down the hall to where she fell... where she faced her mortality. I said a small blessing that it was hardwood and not carpeting. It's odd what stray thoughts go through your mind at a time like this. Perhaps its purpose is to keep you distracted from the reality of the task at hand. As I wiped up the blood, I remembered that one of my bosses from the seventies had a son who took his life by a gunshot to his head. He was found in his mother's completely white bedroom lying on her white bedspread, blood splattered all over the white carpeting and white walls. I imagined a distraught mother trying to clean up all that blood. Why is the family left with the mop-up? Why don't the police have a team come in and do this? Let's get human here.

Friday–July 2nd

Early morning before the workday begins, before I called anyone else in the family, I placed two phone calls, one to her ex-fiancée and one to Justin. They didn't answer. I left messages. The ex-fiancée returned my call. Justin never did. Nor did I hear from any of the other people she had contact with the last few months of her life. Not one call of condolence...not one sympathy card...nothing from any of her so-called new friends. Nor did she receive e-mails from any of those people after July 1. It took only two calls to have the news spread fast among people who weren't supposed to know each other. After all, her obituary didn't appear in the newspaper until the following Tuesday.

Chapter 19

The Aftermath

And so it began, family rushed to Harrisburg from all over—my children, Don's daughter, my sisters. Amongst all this activity is a surprise visitor…a detective…a stranger at this most private moment asking a million questions, asking to inspect the house, invading the privacy of a family in shock, in mourning.

He would call on the phone and ask, "What hand was the knife in?" With the vision still vividly in my mind I replied, "This may sound strange because she was right handed, but the knife was in her left hand." He asked, "Did you ever touch the knife?" I replied, "Yes, several months ago I moved the knife from the top of a chest in the den to the shelf." I recall that as I moved it a chill went through my body and I remember thinking that this knife could kill someone. My unasked questions to him were: "Am I a suspect in this suicide?" "Did he think I murdered my daughter?" "What's going on here?"

The funeral was held on July 8, a week later, a very long, long week later. We had to wait for the autopsy before we could bury her. It was the July 4th holiday weekend. Her body was not released until Tuesday. The body was transported to Erie on Wednesday. Delays. Delays. Delays.

My children accompanied me to the funeral home. They chose the casket; I couldn't bear to go into the coffin room. Cris, my daughter-in-law expressed, "We immediately found the one that was for Melanie. It's purple, her favorite color and it has flowers on it." Saeunn, my other daughter-in-law stated, "It was an unanimous decision; we think you'll like it." They chose the clothes she would wear for her last worldly appearance, the purple and white paisley top we all fondly remembered her wearing. They chose the wording for the prayer cards, which stated, "I'd like the memory of me to be a happy one." They accompanied me to the church and chose the readings and music.

They helped ease the emotional anguish associated with making the final arrangements. Being together, united as a family in laying their sister to rest, helped with their grieving also. They were so strong for my sake, especially Le'Anne. She's the one sibling who could empathize with Melanie's misery.

It was the evening before the funeral. We all gathered at Wayne's house. My friend, Barb, came over with food and the *Songs for the Inner Child* CD. The first track was *How Could Anyone*. Upon hearing the lyrics, we all broke down and sobbed our hearts out. We knew Melanie didn't feel beautiful on the outside and this misconception ate away her confidence like a cancer on the inside. Ed, my oldest son, was sitting on my right. I could hear the deep sorrow in his sobs and put my arms around him. Then we all reached out for each other, huddled, and hugged. We all wondered what more we could have done to help her.

Melanie was buried on a Thursday. One week to the day that was. If I could do it over, could I have been gentler, chosen softer words? I didn't comprehend the full depth of her suffering.

She was buried out of Holy Rosary Church, the church where she was baptized, received her first communion, went to grade school…a place that fondly remembered her. Interment was in Wintergreen Gorge Cemetery…a place where we took our evening walks during her happier childhood days. As we left the cars and started walking toward the gravesite for final prayers, a summer thunder and lightning storm came up out of nowhere. The wind blew so hard I thought the tent would come down. This was a dangerous place to be in such a storm, I didn't want another death to occur so I asked the priest to be brief. As we all rushed back into the safety of our cars, a smile spread across my face at the thought that Melanie was already making her demands in heaven, that she didn't want us to mourn over her gravesite, so she made sure we couldn't.

I knew Mel's spirit would hang around for the funeral. Through my niece Chelsea, who has intuitive abilities, Mel had much to say about what was taking place. She told Chelsea she didn't want us to cry over her body as that was not her. She said in a huff, "It doesn't even look like me." She was right. Her mouth was misshapen, the results of the breathing tube that was left in for the autopsy. All of her hard endeavors, the braces on her teeth for so many years, the jaw operation, the struggle to not look grotesque to children went for naught. The lovely purple and white top was draped up to her neck to cover the dissecting line that ran the length of her body. Even in death, she was denied her external beauty, even when all her muscles were relaxed, all her anguish relinquished to the Creator.

Chelsea continued, "She was pleased with the picture you put in her coffin." It was an angel with dark brown hair dressed in a long black skirt and tube top. A large pink heart took center stage on the top. The angel had large black wings shaped like a butterfly's. The picture had taken up residence on her dresser. When I went into her bedroom, I was drawn to place it in her coffin. Chelsea stated, "She wants you to know that is how she is, not the body in the the casket." Standing at the head of the coffin for the last time surrounded by my remaining children, I prayed for her to leave her cocoon of a physical body and turn into a magnificent butterfly in spirit. I asked that she not remain behind for us. I also placed Lazy dog with her, to accompany her on her journey and protect her as he did when she was a child. Now she is a child of God.

Chelsea disclosed that Mel was not happy with the priest's words. She thought he said something about her singing off tune and was insulted. What he said was, "I was told that Melanie liked to sing, that she received a letter jacket in high school for being in the chorus. It's good to sing, even if it's off tune." Perhaps he was thinking about all those countless Sunday mornings when he would sit in front of the church listening to his dwindling congregation sing. Perhaps he was hearing me singing the opening hymn. Gram said, "It's good to sing. Singing raises the vibration level." She also said, "It's good to laugh. Laughter is healing."

We buried Melanie and then almost immediately left for Lilly Dale, New York, to see an intuitive counselor, Barbara. It was the high season in Lilly Dale, but she made special arrangements to see me in the evening. Why would I seek out an intuitive counselor? Because…Melanie's end just didn't seem to fit the circumstances. Women don't take their lives with a knife to the abdomen. They use pills, slash their wrists, or turn on the car engine; they DO NOT take a knife to the belly.

Barbara had given me a reading before…years ago…in Erie…at the psychic bookstore by Liberty Plaza…Rosanne's shop. Barb is a kind, gentle, soft-spoken woman. She has worked with the Cleveland police and others. I trust she can help us.

As soon as I sat down, I knew I had come too soon as it was hard on Barbara. I apologized. She said, "Not to worry, this is my service to mankind, no need to apologize." Barbara was having a hard time getting Melanie to come through. She would start and then stop. Barbara explained, "It's as if she were banging her head against a wall."

Barb continued, "Melanie had two lives. The one you knew and another one in which she led a very sexually active life. She was two people confined in a body that was letting her down, limiting her communication, her speech, leading her to another way to communicate. Apparently she thought you would not approve of this other life or perhaps she didn't want to share it with you. It was something of her own in which you had no control."

Barbara stated, "Melanie decided when her life would end, no one else. She had control of this one thing. The method of death was to send a clear message to somebody. It was done in the act of a Japanese martyr or to save face. Whatever took place, she went along with it at first. The two men with whom she went to Ocean City are only contact men. There is a big rat behind it somewhere."

I could almost hear her mind's gears churning when all of a sudden an alarmed expression came over her face. "There is something in her bedroom that will incriminate someone. They are thinking of breaking into your house to retrieve it. You must notify the police."

I lamented to Barbara, "It's hard for me to imagine that she would willingly give away $2900 in one week. Each day she withdrew money using her check card and gave it to these men. Why? They held the bank receipts. Why would they keep the withdrawal receipts if the money was willingly given to them?"

Barbara reiterated, "She just isn't coming through, there is some kind of blockage." I offered in a quiet voice, "Perhaps it's because we just buried her today, perhaps that's why." Barbara looked shocked. She said, "My God woman, you're running on fumes!" As soon as I left Barbara's house, we called the detective. I know he must have thought I was some kind of kook, but he said he would take a drive by the house.

Upon our arrival home, the detective paid us one last visit. He stated that Melanie knew these two men for only two weeks at the most. That she had another life that we didn't know about, a sexually active life. He said there were pictures. He stated that through his interviews (he couldn't tell us who he interviewed), it appears she did everything willingly, including giving her money away. Of course this would be said; the only person who could refute them was dead. He said that she had been really sick (as in mental) for the last year. Who could have said this? These people didn't know her then. Her death was ruled a suicide and the case closed.

The detective did reveal that Andrew was like Melanie, disabled and that he stuttered. He said the first thing out of Andrew's mouth was, "I have a right to a lawyer." If this man were not guilty of anything, why would he think he needed a lawyer? The detective continued, "The longer Andrew talked the more he stuttered; in the end it was hard to understand him." My psychologist stated that stuttering is a sign of anxiety. As his anxiety increased, so did the stuttering. We both wondered why? What was he hiding? The detective couldn't talk to Justin because he was away for the holiday. No kidding, he took a holiday on a dead woman's money. I often wondered if Justin's family had an "in" with the police. Why was he exonerated so quickly?

The detective explained that Mel tried to take her life a couple of months before by swallowing pills, but got scared and stopped. Since I don't know the source of this revelation, if in fact it is true, why would she then take a knife to herself, an act that requires much more courage than downing a bunch of pills? I found nothing in her e-mails that spoke of this attempt.

We were led to believe that the detective had talked to her ex-fiancé, but he told us this did not occur. There was nobody in her e-mails that was there a year ago. Who would say this about her? The e-mails, written correspondence, and items I recovered were from people we didn't know or meet. There were just too many inconsistencies between what the detective revealed and the Melanie we knew and loved.

If she gave away the money freely, why did Justin hold all her ATM bank receipts? When reviewing her bank history that night, I commanded, "Let me see all your bank receipts." She replied, "Justin has them." When I asked why he would be keeping the receipts, she didn't answer right away. Later, she said something about going back down there and giving her ID number because the machine never spit out the $400. This reason didn't make sense. She would have heard from the bank if the ATM didn't balance out.

Justin's whole story that night didn't make sense. He stated, "The $900 is for a hotel for the holiday weekend." I retorted, "Don and I travel a lot, and we never had to pay that much for a hotel for two days." He reiterated that it was a holiday. Then he said, "We're booking the room online." I know that online booking requires a credit card, not cash. Whom is he trying to fool? He also said they were staying at the same campground as before, so his stories didn't match.

The very next day after Justin's noxious visit, the day I left the phone message...we went out to the garage in the afternoon and discovered a new tent still in its box, unopened. We didn't recall seeing it before and wondered how it got there? Going through Mel's receipts, we discovered that she had purchased the tent on the day of her death. Did Justin have possession of it and decided to return it?

We talked to the ex-fiancée. He stated, "The police never talked to him." I asked if they talked to his family. He replied, "No." He also stated that to his knowledge she had never tried to take her life, he didn't agree that she was "mental" that last year. He also asked if he could have the engagement ring back!

About a week after her death, his brother's ex-girlfriend was at a house where Jessica (the person whose phone bill Melanie paid) was talking about Melanie's death and the $2900. At that point, only four people knew this exact amount, Justin, the detective, my husband and I. How did Jessica know the exact amount? Justin said he didn't know this Jessica. More inconsistencies.

Everyone in Melanie's life at the time of her death seemed to be centered around this woman Jessica. Mel met Jessica online. A man in jail named Nick was sending Melanie letters at Jessica's address. Why did Melanie pay Jessica's phone bill? Did Melanie meet Andrew or Justin through Jessica? How did Jessica find out about the $2900? Why didn't I hear from Jessica upon Melanie's death?

My head is spinning. There are too many unanswered questions, too many conflicting stories. Is this the way it is with all suicides?

My son, Wayne, must have been experiencing similar emotions for he decided to visit a friend, an old eccentric monk originating from Italy. Wayne needed to discuss Melanie's death with him. The first thing out of the monk's mouth was, "Who went to see the witches?" The monk told Wayne, "Melanie would go into the light on Saturday at 11 PM." He instructed, "Have your family say prayers to assist in her transition." I called several of my spiritual friends to start a prayer network. At the appointed time, Don, Le'Anne, and I sat on the spot where Mel's spirit left her body. We lit a white candle, proceeded to say goodbye, and sent her on her way with all our love and prayers.

In the middle of the night, Wayne's son, Markus (Mel's godson), awoke crying and screaming. Saeunn rushed into his room to find him banging on his bedroom window crying out, "Take me with you, I want to go with you!" When she questioned him the next morning, he said, "Aunt Mellie was sitting on my bed. She was singing to me. She told me goodbye." I took this as affirmation that she indeed had transitioned.

Journal Entry–July 12, 2004

Today we went to the Credit Union to close out Melanie's accounts.

I didn't want to take a chance that one of those scumbags might try to withdraw what was left. I asked about the four-hundred dollar withdrawal that Melanie stated didn't come out of the machine. I also asked if they could tell me the times of her withdrawals. They stated that there should be pictures because she did a couple of withdrawals from that location. They are to call me tomorrow.

Saeunn called. She had a dream last night. She recalled, "In the dream I was in the viewing room of the funeral home when I saw Melanie's arm move. At first, I thought it was just a muscle spasm, then Mel's whole body moved and she said she was not dead. I wanted to get a psychologist to help Mel deal with the situation, but she told me she was okay; that she had her spiritual group to help her. Then the dream went on...something about Iraq...then back to Melanie holding a baby, saying how little and light the baby was. Then Melanie said she had to get on with her new job."

A week later while talking to my niece, Chelsea, she related, "There is more Melanie wanted you to know when you are ready to accept it." Then Mel said, "No, that I would blame myself and she didn't want that to happen." Could it be that Melanie was pregnant? Don said that thought had crossed his mind also. Could the two men have been helping her to get an abortion and that's where the money went? Could the detective have found this out and that's why he didn't think it necessary to pursue anyone. Barbara mentioned

108

something about money for an operation. I must get the autopsy report, get to the truth, and solve all that I can. Deal with it...then heal.

Journal Entry–July 15, 2004

Two weeks down...a lifetime to go. It's been a hectic two weeks. The first one spent in Erie preparing for her funeral and the second week spent tying up loose ends. It's been frantic, what I need is some quiet time by myself. Not Don...not anyone.

Everyone is saying I am doing well. I think I am doing too well; am I still numb? I LOST MY DAUGHTER. A part of me has been torn out and has died with her. Perhaps that's why I'm still numb. Like her, I'm bleeding on the inside. It still doesn't seem possible.

Today, Don and I went grocery shopping. Usually most of the cart was taken up with food for Melanie. Don would say, "Do you think Melanie would like this?" I would say, "Don't forget to pick up two cans of chicken for her." It was so strange today. Both of us mentioned that we have no "Melanie" items in the cart. Guess this is a string of *firsts* post-Melanie.

I've made an appointment for grief counseling with a psychologist. It's more for my husband and daughter. Who knows? Perhaps it will benefit me also. I've cleaned her personal items out of the hall bathroom to make it "neutral" for when we have guests. Her bedroom door remains closed. I can't bear the thought of cleaning it out yet.

Journal Entry–July 17, 2004

Yesterday, I went to see my friend Jacki, who lives just across the border in Maryland. I thought some Reiki healing could help my totally depleted body.

I felt so weak and was concerned that in this weakened state I could be letting lower entities attack my psyche. We talked for a while about how it happened and what I am thinking of doing. When I mentioned about going to the FBI, Jackie said, "Look, I have chills all over my body. I think this is a confirmation of what you should do."

Because I was finding it difficult to "be present," it took over three hours for Jacki to do "her thing." It was the first time in weeks I felt the least bit relaxed. I didn't sleep well the night before; I was up at 4 AM. I wonder when Mel will come to me in my dreams? She has already visited Saeunn and Markus to let them know she is all right.

Today, Don picked up the computers and Mel's personal items from the police station. A deputy coroner who was present at the autopsy spoke to Don. Don asked about the possibility of her being pregnant. The deputy coroner responded with, "There was no indication of her being pregnant." He also said, "I have never seen such destructive rage in all my years in this profession." I told Don, "Rage is something you take out against another person; this action is more the result of self-loathing."

Everything on Melanie's computer had been erased by the police. Nothing was left, not even my old files. Then I remembered that she also used my computer. I sat down at mine and read the e-mails from her last two or three days of life. From what she said about Don and me, I can't see that our words that night would have caused her to take that drastic of an action. She thought we were "woosies" and stated that our words don't scare her. Then, what did scare her enough to make her take her life?

The e-mails aren't easy for a mother to read. There was the sweet Melanie that she presented to her extended family. There was the defiant Melanie that she was with me as in, "I'm not going to do anything you ask or want. I won't argue with you, but I won't do it." Then there is this third Melanie…the one I didn't know. Did she enjoy sex that much? Was it a power thing with her? Was it a way to receive acceptance from others? Or was it the only way she was still on equal footing?

Pictures were e-mailed to her, but I couldn't open them. The detective said something about pictures. Did he see them? Did she erase everything from her computer or did the police? If they did, why? Was there something incriminating about one of them?

Don finally left me alone for a few hours yesterday. Was he concerned about me taking my life? That thought has not crossed my mind. It felt good to be alone in the house.

A few years ago, Don and I took a trip to Ireland. As we drove around the country, Don was excited for me to see Loch Gur. He had been there before and thought I would be interested in the folklore surrounding this area and especially, a stone circle. The circle was erected around 2500 BC. We had to walk through a cow pasture to reach it. The cows were grazing just a few feet away and we had to dodge numerous cow patties. I was concerned we might frighten them or more likely, that they would frighten us! Don walked back to the car so I could be alone to walk the circle. I touched each of the

113 megaliths as I made the round and gathered several small stones off the ground that had peeled away from the larger sentinels. I also plucked a leaf from each of the four large trees that stood right outside the circle marking the four directions and gave thanks for having received their permission to do so. Gram said, "We must ask permission before we take and give gratitude that we are allowed."

On the floor of my office sits a stone casting of four indigenous women with long braids down their backs, their linked arms forming a circle. In the middle of this circle is a small pot. I took one of the stones and a piece from each of the leaves I brought back from Ireland and put them into the maidens' pot, and then placed the pot in the center of the room. The lit leaves furnished a smoldering purifying "smudge" while I said a prayer. Then I took down my medicine drum from its place on the shelf, the drum that was used to keep the heartbeat of the seventh Peace Elders Council...

I sat in my office/medicine room and drummed for a while. The beat started out weak, but soon I was drumming as hard as I could. Banging on the drum, I walked throughout the whole downstairs. Banging the drum at the spot where she plunged that damn knife into her stomach and just as quickly pulled it out. Banging the drum at the steps where her blood fell in drops, banging the drum in the hall where she took a few steps towards me, banging the drum at the spot where she collapsed, too weak to do anything but breathe. I banged and banged and banged, over and over and over. Banging the drum harder and harder and harder...trying to rid myself of all the pent-up anger over such a senseless act. What were those low life men threatening her with? What truth should I be told?

Then I went upstairs and started banging the drum in her room. Something told me to stop. I put the drum down on her bed and started looking. For what? The item that Barbara said we would find if we went over her room with a fine tooth comb, the item that somebody was thinking of breaking into our house to retrieve, something in her room that would incriminate...who?

I must say that between the drumming and the Reiki session, I feel a little more at ease today. I can look at and touch Melanie's things without becoming anxious inside.

o o o o o

Today, Le'Anne and Morgen came over for the afternoon and stayed for supper. Don put up the blue elephant splash pool. Morgen played while the three of us sat and watched. She so enjoyed the water sprinkling out of the elephant's nose. It was a good distraction; how healing a child's laughter can be!

I asked if Morgen has awakened and cried in the middle of the night for Melanie. She hasn't, but she has been going around their house looking for Melanie. Although Morgen is just a few weeks short of her third birthday; I sense she knows Melanie is gone for good. Mel was the first person she looked for when entering our house. Morgen always went straight into my office to retrieve Mel's phone to play house. Mel was usually sitting at my computer. Morgen no longer asks where Melanie is or where is her car. She still talks about Mel, but doesn't ask for her. Today, when Morgen saw my prescription bottles, she said they were Aunt Melanie's medicine.

It has been my experience that when somebody close to you passes on, he/she will come to you in your dreams to let you know he/she is all right. There is a new moon phase tonight. I await Melanie's visit to let ME know all is well with her, that she has moved into the light. I love her so. I always will.

Journal Entry–July 19, 2004

I went to the doctor's today. He said, "I don't think you are ready to go back to work. You need at least two more weeks." He continued, "You are a prime candidate for family medical leave, I know so many people abuse it, but it was made for people like you."

The doctor philosophized, "We live in a microwave world. We have learned to expect things instantly, but emotions and relationships are not like that. In this technical world of having it all at our fingertips and getting it done and over with, our spiritual needs still require time, including time to grieve and heal. You must give yourself more time to grieve, to really feel the pain, not push it aside to deal with other things such as work issues. I advise you to have at least two grief counseling sessions under your belt before going back to work." Last Friday, I felt ready to go back. Today, I was relieved that I didn't have to.

Under stress, my bowels usually become blocked and my blood pressure elevates. Once the funeral was over, I've had no problem with my bowels and my blood pressure is 130/83. That's a good reading for me. I feel guilty about this.

With Melanie gone, my emotional load has lessened. It was quite difficult to see her suffer constant neck and back pain. The pain kept her from sleeping. It was quite difficult to see her suffer in silence when the engagement ended. It took away her future, her self-esteem. She would have nothing to do with counseling. It surely must have been difficult with people not understanding what you are saying, people thinking you are mentally retarded because of your speech, children staring at a body that can't respond and reflect what you are inside. She must have felt trapped in more ways than one. I can understand. So can Le'Anne, for she suffers also.

Journal Entry–July 21, 2004

I went to bed around 9:30 PM last night to watch TV, read, and hopefully fall asleep. It didn't work, so I got up around midnight and made some lemon bars.

I called a man in the FBI who went to high school with my son, Ed. He had talked to us around a year ago about a case where a man was using the Internet to entice underage girls to have sex with him. The man was eventually caught in a sting operation. The detective said, "Funny, the timing of your call. The man is being sentenced today."

I asked him if something of this nature could have happened with Melanie. He thought I was looking for closure. He stated in a matter of fact tone that, "If indeed, Melanie, was being blackmailed/extorted, you have no proof other than her testimony, which is now impossible." Barbara had told me that if the police go through her room with a fine tooth comb they would find something that would incriminate the ones who are at the root of her taking her life, not the two men who were used to lure Melanie but the "fat rat" who is behind it all. I called Barbara to see if she could "see" where or what to look for. So far, she hasn't returned my call.

One of the books I'm reading on grief states that if there is unfinished business such as saying "I'm sorry," then you must find a way to express your emotions, good or bad, to begin to heal. It suggested writing a letter to your loved one. So here goes…

Dear Melanie,

Nobody could love you more than me—your mother. I was 35 when I became pregnant with you after going through a miscarriage a few months before.

I was attending Penn State Erie and had a full plate of responsibilities. Your father didn't like me attending school and locking myself in the bedroom to study. He wanted/needed the time I devoted to school. Perhaps, he thought it would change me and I would not want him, so he wanted another child to bind me to him. I agreed to his wants, became pregnant again, and quit school.

The early months of your pregnancy drained my energy, so did having a three-year-old girl and two boys in grade school. School was hard for me that year. I was having problems with College Algebra and Spanish as both were scheduled in the same semester.

I never regretted having you. In fact, I wanted you very much. It was the night of a full moon when my water broke, but there were no labor pains. The doctor asked me to go to the hospital the next morning so he could induce labor. Again, nothing happened. Finally, in the early evening he decided to do a C-section. It seems you were obstinate even back then, displaying a mind of your own. I saw you being taken to the nursery in a heated bed with the placenta in a plastic bag beside you. I always thought that was strange, but never received an explanation.

For the first three months of your life, I constantly held you, for you would cry if anyone else tried. You were an adorable eight-pound, nine-ounce bundle of joy and such a cute young child. One of my favorite pictures is that of you in your kindergarten graduation dress standing under the big oak tree in our backyard. Your back was toward the camera to show off your long tresses and your head was turned slightly to show your face.

For your junior prom, I bought you a vintage red gown in England. There are pictures of you in that dress, with a big red bump on your forehead, the bump that activated the Ataxia. If only you had worn your seatbelt like the other girls in the car, your life would have been different, you would still be alive, but you ARE NOT.

Flash forward to your last day. I decided to stay home from work and clean the house. Ann and Jim were coming for the weekend and I was not prepared, so I called off sick. I did feel sick or out of sorts. I had to push myself to do some cleaning. You knew we were getting company, yet you didn't offer to help me. You were at the computer or watching TV. I needed help, but you didn't offer and I was not going to ask. At times, it's just easier to do it yourself.

Sometime in the afternoon, I saw you walk across the lawn, purse in hand. I asked where you had been. I was dumb in giving you a response when I asked if you went for a walk. You said, "Yeah." A while later you asked if you could use my car to go to Target. Call it mother's intuition or whatever, while you were gone I read a few of your e-mails and didn't like what I saw. I left my purse in the front seat of my car and now I was concerned that someone might steal it.

When you returned, I asked if you wanted to open another savings account and put your extra money away for a vacation, emergency, or a rainy day. You agreed, so I asked how much you had left after purchasing the car, I recalled it should be around $4,000. You called the credit union to get the balance, $1,400. I asked how this can be true and went into your account history to check your withdrawals. Within the last week, you had withdrawn $2,900; $950 in just one day.

When I found out you had given the majority of it to Justin and Andrew, I asked you to go online and get it back. Justin agreed to return the $500 he still had, Andrew had the other $400. When Justin pulled into the driveway to return the money, the police were just a few minutes behind.

Justin handed over the money, along with a few bank receipts from your Ocean City, Maryland trip. I had him sign a written con-tract stating he would repay you $500 the first of each month until you were fully reimbursed. He told you to get online with Andrew and see if he would confess that he had the $400 so Justin could then take some legal action to regain the portion Andrew owed. When Justin went to the car, you pushed past Don to get to Justin. What did you say to him?

Justin spoke about how oddly Andrew treated you on the trip. I asked why you would want to go again next week with somebody who treated you so badly. I said that once your money ran out they would be gone, that they were using you.

When Justin left, you ran into Don's office trying to get to Andrew on the computer. You said you HAD to talk to Andrew. I took you into the house and told you not to talk to Andrew. Don followed us into the house. I said that giving away this amount of money was the last straw; I cannot take it anymore. I told you to withdraw the rest of your money and purchase a bus ticket, that I wanted you out of the house TONIGHT.

I asked Don to get the CPU out of the basement room as I started to unhook the one in my office. As Don took the CPU out to his office in the garage, he stopped by the door and said if there is one thing he cannot stand it is a liar, because you can never trust them to say the truth, ever. I agreed with him, stating that you had been lying to me for weeks, maybe even months. I can't remember what else I said, if anything. I was quite fed up with your behavior.

This is when you ran out of the room and took the action that not only took your life, but also changed the lives of everyone who loved you. Mellie, from your new perspective, you must know that I love you very much, that I forgive you for that other part of your life that was so radically different from the Melanie of our family. I can understand your need for acceptance from your peers and this desperate attempt to fit in, only it was with the wrong crowd. I think in your heart you knew this.

What led to your desperation that you no longer wanted to live? Was it my words? We had arguments before when I said you had to leave. Just as there was only so much you could endure, the same was true for me. To watch you suffer emotional and physical pain each day, to watch you become isolated except for your family, to see you deteriorate more and more each week, weighed heavy on my heart, on my soul. I could feel your pain, but you would not reach out, would not acknowledge your feelings to me.

I am so sorry if the words I said were the impetus to your decision. I'm so very, very sorry. Just as I forgive you the things that the "other" Melanie was led to do, I ask that you forgive my words to you that night. I know you may find it hard to believe, but I did have your best interest in mind. I could not stand by and let those scum bags prey on you anymore. I was a momma bear protecting her young. Now, the Creator is your protector.

Please forgive me.

Love,

Mom

Journal Entry–July 23, 2004

Wayne is 33 today.

Don and I arrived home simultaneously in our separate cars. He was just in front of me as we drove up the hill. There was a white Altima parked not quite in front of our house, but still in front of our property. A young attractive woman was sitting in the car. Was she waiting for us? I thought it strange and stared at her as we drove by. She stared back. As we pulled into our garage, she got out of her car and walked down the hill.

Don watched to see where she went. He thought she went into the driveway two houses down. He started cooking some meat on the grill which sits on the side deck of the house. I asked him to watch for her return. About 8 or 10 minutes later she knocked on our door. She was in her early twenties, blonde hair, wearing cropped jeans and a red jacket that said "Save the Children" above the left hand pocket. She started talking about children in poverty, and she wanted to ask us some survey questions. I replied, "Look, we had a tragedy in our family and I'm in no mood to answer surveys." She giggled and said, "I hope things work out fine." She giggled…

After leaving our house, she got in her car and pulled away. Why didn't she go to the other houses by us? We were the last house she visited. I got into my car and drove to the end of the driveway to see if she was still in the neighborhood. She had driven further up the hill, skipping several homes in between. I then spotted her walking up to another house. Don said I was being silly, "If she was there to trouble us, why she would bother going to the other houses?" I replied, "If I were in her shoes, I would have, just to establish an alibi for being in the neighborhood." I was not trustful. Will I ever trust a stranger again?

Yesterday was my first appointment for grief counseling with Family Services. To me the man looked as if he had been working with the agency since his youth. He reminded me of a burnt out state worker, not a good sign! I didn't like him, but I'll see what Don and Le think. He said it appears I'm doing well with my grieving.

Wednesday we had lunch with a couple who are friends of Don. The woman's first husband had hung himself. She wanted to provide some comfort to me, but it turned into a reliving of that horrible time for her. She did more talking then listening. That's all right, she must have needed to talk about it and I provided the opportunity. Even in our deepest despair, we can still help others. That evening Don broke down. He cried out, "If only she had come to me, I would have helped her." He had loved her as a daughter. He had remained strong for me, but it took a toll on his emotional and physical health. It's good he finally broke down.

Tonight, Don and I had words. He started in on Le'Anne and her messiness. I retorted, "Now that Melanie's gone, are you going to continuously pick on Le like you did Mel? My girls will never be like your children or like my boys." I begged, "Please leave her alone. I don't want to lose another child." Why does her messiness bother him so? His office is just as messy. Well...not quite. I don't have the patience for his nagging at this moment. Just how important is it in the bigger picture?

Journal Entry–July 25, 2004

Today is Morgen's third birthday.

Le'Anne had tears in her eyes when I picked them up to bring them to our house. This is the first family celebration without Melanie. Morgen no longer asks for her, she just whispers that Melanie is an angel now. I know the Creator is loving and I know he takes good care of my daughter. She rests now, but we don't have peace yet. I'm still in the process of going through her room; not clearing out her clothes yet, just combing every nook and cranny for anything that might provide us with a clue. I found phone numbers, directions, addresses, and letters from a man who is/was in the York County Jail. I need to find out what for. I did find something that may prove fruitful in the future?

Yesterday, the bill for the funeral came in the mail. I went into my office to pay it and broke down into sobs and moans. The anxiety and the tightness in my chest returned. So, this is how grieving goes, you're going along fine and then it hits.

They say six months and two years are bad periods for grieving, that it all seems new again. It's about six months since Mel's engagement was called off. Did her pain come back anew? Was she suffering in silence? Now we all suffer.

Don and I took a ride by Justin's house yesterday evening. He lives with his parents in a subdivision just minutes away. Does he suffer guilt knowing that Mel took her life minutes after he left? Will he suffer guilt the rest of his life like her family does over our loss? When he marries and has a daughter, will he worry about her because there will be men like him out there, men who prey on the weak? Yes, he will have a long life to remember his part in this tragedy.

What about that other worm, Andrew? Will his stuttering grow worse until nobody will be able to understand him? Will he become a victim of prey? What goes around comes around. How will the Universe pay them back? What about this man who was in prison? I found out he was charged with underage rape. What's his role in her ending? Who was in our house when we were in France?

I try very hard not to have bad thoughts about them because I don't want or need anything negative on a spiritual level coming back around to me. I trust the Universe to deal with these men. I have to forgive myself for my role, for saying she could not live with us anymore, for saying she lied to me so many times I couldn't trust her anymore, for saying the truth, not knowing she didn't have the inner strength to handle everything that was coming down on her. Will I ever know the whole story…the whole truth?

Journal Entry–August 7, 2004

I had to not write for awhile. I had to not read about grieving for awhile. I had to take a break from all of it for awhile…but found it impossible.

Guess I must be in an angry stage, angry that I had to go back to work half days starting this past Tuesday and had to listen to all my co-workers welcome me back, listen to them say how sorry they are, that they can't even imagine. I want to scream, "Don't even try to imagine, don't put that thought out into the ethers. Just blow it away." How many people know just how powerful thoughts are, that it just takes a millisecond to birth a thought into the physical? Is that not what Melanie did, in her fit of rage?

Getting back into the routine of work is very difficult. Work hasn't changed, but I have. I am no longer *that* person. I no longer have fire; I'm just ashes going through the motions. I worked to provide for the girls. Mel is gone, Le is doing OK. She and Morgen have medical benefits. Work is not the same because I AM NOT THE SAME.

My supervisor gave me the name of another counselor he thought might be helpful. He said to take more time off if needed; he seems very understanding. I have one year and three months until I can retire. Can I last that long at this job that causes me to be constipated? No kidding! All the time I was off work, no problems. The week I start back, I'm back to being plugged up! I am reminded of Twylah's philosophy. What won't I eliminate from my life? What is no longer growing corn? The only plausible answer…my job.

Don could use some emotional support from his family. Do they realize that he took it badly also? He needs some downtime. I worry about him. He's 81. The funeral affected his physical health. At the funeral parlor, his leg swelled up so much that he wasn't able to stand by my side. I can't lose him…I need his emotional support right now. He's my rock, my pillar of strength, my security.

Today has been a very blue day for me. I have cried on and off all day. Is Melanie aware of the mess she has left behind? How we still grieve for her? The books that deal with grief and suicide don't quite hit the mark with me. They talk about the stages of grief but don't really capture how it feels to go through these stages.

Take the anger stage. I get angry over the smallest things. I'm angry that she is not here to help us with the DVD, that she is not here to watch over Le'Anne when Don and I want to escape for a weekend, that she is not here when I get home from work.

Why did she have to take her life right after we had words? She knows that the day after, when our emotions have settled down, we would sit down and talk about it. She changed the lives of all of us…left gaping holes in all of us.

I read a book by James Van Praagh in which he states that those who commit suicide most likely have also done so in a previous life. It's because they reincarnate too soon and are not strong enough to handle the Earth's vibration. This rings true with Melanie. As a preschooler, she was very, very sensitive and seemed to get out of sorts very easily, as if things were too much for her system. In the long term, I guess this turned out to be true. I send her my love each day and encourage her to take time to heal on the other side. I want her to be successful so she doesn't have to go through this scenario again and again. It's too painful for all of us.

Journal Entry–August 16, 2004

Six weeks down the road (has it only been six weeks?), it feels like this heavy mantle of grieving has been with me so much longer.

I didn't go to work today. My gut was churning like crazy with anticipation of work. My supervisor said to stay home when things get to be too much. I'm taking his advice.

Janet, my friend from England, called last night and we talked for a couple of hours. She said Melanie is where she needs to be and most likely is trying to communicate with me. It's me that is not open to her communication because I am still bogged down in the why and wherefores. Once we get the autopsy report, once we decide whether to hire a private investigator, or once we move towards closure on her physical life, I will become more open and will be able to "hear" her.

Work is crumbling down upon me. The present bureau director is a pompous ass as is his new executive assistant. Why does she feel threatened and want to get rid of me? I could mentor her in the ways of the field staff… smooth the transition as I am respected in the field. I'm ready to take a back seat; so to speak, I'll be retiring in a year. It seems my supervisor and the director argues over me every day. I was advised that in order to get out of their firing range I should turn over all the training to her, since she felt she was the expert. He said I could become his executive assistant as he has more than he could handle. I said I felt this arrangement would divide the bureau into two camps, and at this level it would not help the bureau as a whole.

Unless the situation at work changes, I don't think I can make it to my retirement age of 60, which is next November. My stress level needs to be reduced; life needs to become more simplified. My memory needs to return to a somewhat normal state. I need to remove any unnecessary complications. It's hard to focus on *everyday* work matters; I can't even begin to focus on *future* goals. It's time for somebody else to take over. I informed my trainers of the decision to step down, so they know ahead of time what to expect and to make their own decisions in regards to working with a new leader.

Don and I talked about the situation at work and other things over the weekend. It's quite difficult for me to continue to live in this house where my daughter's life ended. To pass the trail of blood, although weeks removed in the physical, it's still there in my mind, haunting me emotionally. I purposely don't walk on the spot where she fell; it's as if I'm stepping on her. We decided to start to look at properties in Western Pennsylvania.

Journal Entry–August 22, 2004

It feels as if I have regressed back to July 2. The pain only seems to intensify–not lessen.

We picked up the autopsy report Wednesday night so we could ask for any medical clarification regarding what it contained at my doctor's appointment on Thursday. Upon reading the report, it was a shock to learn that Melanie had stabbed herself more than once. There were two entrance wounds, with three wound paths, meaning that she pulled the knife out part way and then plunged it back in. She had severed both the main artery and vein.

The report states there were 30 cc of bloody fluid in the pericardial sac (heart). There was a liter of blood in the left chest, a few hundred cc of blood in the right chest, and there was greater than 500 cc of blood in the abdominal cavity. The report also states there is anthracotic (black) pigment in her lungs. Is this the leftovers from her botched surgery?

I couldn't go to work on Thursday, as I was too emotionally distraught over the multiple wounds. Why didn't the emergency medical technicians tell us about multiple wounds? Why didn't the police or the detective? Why didn't the doctor at the hospital? Why did we have to wait six weeks to find out?

How could anyone do that to oneself? It's so hard for me to comprehend. What courage…desperation…self-loathing….rage…it took to do this to herself. Why did she choose such a violent way to die? Did she want to make sure she wouldn't survive? My pain is so deep; it is almost unbearable to think that I, her mother, could also have contributed to taking it? Was it my words that pushed her over the edge?

Don and I went away for the weekend to attend a seminar at Lilly Dale, a spiritual retreat in Western New York. It turned out to be a disappointment. The next day we attended a lecture in the auditorium where I was suddenly overtaken with grief and started crying. Because we were sitting so far up front in the audience, we couldn't leave without disturbing everyone. Therefore, we just sat there while I cried. Even though my head was down, it seemed as if the man giving the lecture was delivering a message just for me. Every time I had a swell of emotion come over me, I could hear his voice falter. He started talking about the environment and Native Americans; soon he was talking about hugging trees and lying on the ground flat out to let Mother Earth absorb our emotions.

Of course…this is what I have done in the past…on Twylah's land. Why in all my torment did I forget this? After the speaker finished and before the next one started, we left and headed back to the B&B.

That evening we were invited to attend a cowboy cookout in the field behind the bed and breakfast where we were staying. The other guests and the owners of the B&B had been horseback riding before dinner. We all gathered around two tables that had been set-up on a rise in the field. It appeared as if we were centered on the land in a clearing that was surrounded by tall grasses followed by the trees forming the border. The horses were tethered nearby. All the food was cooked over an open fire. Gram always said an open fire is healing, as being in nature is healing. All had a good time—and for a few hours, Melanie was not foremost in my mind.

When we arrived home, I had Le over for dinner and told her about the autopsy. We both went outside and lay on the earth. We sang a few songs, gave thanks, sent Mel our love, and then continued with life…

Journal Entry—September 8, 2004

This past weekend was the Labor Day holiday. Don, Melanie, and I had advance tickets for the American Idol concert in Hershey. This was the only TV show all three of us watched together. We made a big deal about it, reminding each other when it was coming on, discussing the singers, making a fun time of it. I just couldn't go to the concert without Mel, so I sent Le and Don.

I have been feeling "flat" for the past five or six days, very weepy also. Today, these feelings lifted. Was it because of the holiday and the concert? My psychologist said to remember that the heart feels first, then the mind catches up at some point. At some point, they will get together and that is when acceptance begins.

We finally connect with a private investigator. After relating some of the details to him, he stated he could not get involved in criminal matters, but made the following suggestions. Talk to the ex-fiancée to see if he can fill you in on the past months about Melanie's mental state or anything else. I knew this day would come, but wanted to wait to see if the investigator wanted to talk to him first. Get your ducks in a row, and then take your suspicions to the district attorney to have them conduct an investigation. Go as a grieving mother, a taxpayer, a voter. If none of this works, walk out and tell them you're going to the newspaper.

He said, "It sounds like somebody had a psychological hold on your daughter. That even if we should not have enough to press criminal charges, the police may already be investigating these people, and I may be able to provide a missing piece—that if this is a ring or some kind of cult—it must be prevented from happening to somebody else."

o o o o o

There has been a turnaround at work. Thanks Creator. I asked to be removed from heading staff development. I'm tired of the antics. It's not worth the stress. It's time to pass it off, fold my cards and blow it away.

The first day of the transition, my replacement (the new executive assistant) walked out of my office after 30 seconds, pissed off because things were not in the format she thought they should be in. She has been bad-mouthing me for several months to the bureau director. That evening I sent my supervisor an e-mail requesting a meeting in the morning with the four of us—to clear the air. Upon entering his office the next morning to see if the meeting was set-up, he chased me out, said I should talk to the director by myself. I walked into the director's office and asked for a few minutes of his time.

I stated that I thought there was a misunderstanding concerning the transition. He bellowed, "You bet there is a misunderstanding. I'm getting calls every day about how badly I'm treating you. I'm supposed to be removing you from your job. The union even called and I told them it was none of their business—you're in management!" I responded back, "I had no idea all this was taking place. Is there anything I can do to stop the rumors?" He said, "I'll take care of it." In a way, it was nice to hear that people were concerned, but they are not helping me. I can't afford to be fired!

I told him that I didn't think he knew the whole story about my daughter's death; then I proceeded to tell him...he didn't know. The whole time I am talking, I'm crying and at times, I could see his eyes misting up. He proceeded to tell me, "I have friends that went through something similar and I can tell you that this is something that will be with you for the rest of your life. I'm sure your words did not cause her to take her life." I said, "I think my replacement has unrealistic expectations of what my unit's about." He responded, "Don't worry, I'll talk to her. You must get well."

All the while he was being kind to my face; he was working in the background to get me downgraded. I think it is the work of the executive assistant; she doesn't want me to be at the same pay grade as her. I think she is also trying to get herself promoted…

Last Thursday, we had another transition meeting. It was the complete opposite of the first one. In a short time, I'll be out of the training business and she will no longer be able to put blame on me. I will be out of her firing range.

Journal Entry–September 11, 2004

It was three years ago today when the World Trade Center towers fell. I'm sure all the families of those who were lost are still grieving the tragedy. Their pain probably compares to mine…ours.

I have started pulling together a cohesive package to take to the district attorney's office to see if they will investigate further.

Today, Melanie's ex-fiancée came over to discuss the break-up. According to him, it was a clean break at the end of January. They didn't communicate after he brought over her stuff. He stated that the two months preceding the break-up, it seemed as if they were always fighting. He said it seemed she intentionally wanted to argue. I stated that she was that way with me also. His story seems to go along with what she had told me. There were some things she didn't like regarding his home situation. I always told her the situation was not going to change. She would have to live with it or let it go.

Journal Entry–September 20, 2004

Hurricane Ivan took a quick trip through the mid-state this weekend. Like any wild party when it's over, the hurricane left behind a mess—enough of one that the governor closed the state offices in the Capitol Complex today for all nonessential function employees. This very nonessential function state worker has at least the morning off.

In the afternoon, I drove to State College to attend an employer relations session that we contracted with an outside vendor; it's one of the modules in the CareerLink Specialist Formal Training Plan that is linked to probation. The formal training plan and Workforce Professional Certification are a few of the accomplishments I set in place while working in central office.

How funny? We think work is so important; we dedicate all our time to it. Yes, sometimes at the expense of our family. We only fool ourselves into thinking that what we do is important. Important for how long? A new administration comes in and anyone who was important has been let go, transferred to another bureau/agency, or given such a menial position that they lose all the fire in their belly.

I will be out of the staff development business by October 8th . Soon, the new head will have no ideas and suggestions coming from me; she'll be on her own. Mark my words…pretty soon she will alienate everyone across the state.

I need to pull the materials together to go to the DA's office. It takes such an emotional investment that I have to build up to it…

Talking to Mel's ex-fiancée last week was good for me. I now know that Melanie did not demonstrate to him any of those questionable characteristics that the detective was trying to paint of her last year on Earth.

Grieving is such hard work…and it is work…if you want to get beyond it and live life again…in a new way. I think of her every day. It may be watery eyes for about ten seconds as a memory flickers across my mind. I give into it, cry, and then say to myself, "Okay, time to move on." I woke up this morning and a picture of the blood on our wood floor flashed through my mind. Why?

Saturday, I went through her off-season clothes that are stored in the basement and got them ready for Good Will. I'm not ready to part with the treasures from her childhood yet. I'm not ready to wipe away every physical reminder. She did exist…she was/is loved…and she will be remembered.

Yesterday, without any prior intentions of doing so, I purchased new bed linens for her room. I keep saying that by Christmas, her room will be cleared out and ready for guests. I don't want to change anything in her room until I go to the DA's office in case something is needed.

As I transition into my "non-duties" which consist of busy work others don't have time for, I prepare to retire in the spring instead of waiting for my 60th birthday when I would have full medical benefits for the rest of my life. Because I suffer from the winter blues, my psychologist doesn't want me to quit until spring. She said I should have something to fall back on–not just sit in the house and do nothing. She's concerned I may fall into a deep depression.

We decided to put the house up for sale in February and will go to the Laurel Highlands this weekend to start the process of house hunting.

We're going to Edinboro the first weekend in October to celebrate Markus' and Gretchen's birthdays. While there, I'll get a headstone for Melanie's grave. I guess it's more for us. I know she doesn't care.

Journal Entry–October 4, 2004

We flew to Erie this weekend to celebrate my grandchildren's birthdays and choose the headstone for Mel's grave. Le picked out green granite. We're having Mel's tattoo inscribed on the stone along with these words: I'd like to leave an afterglow of smiles. Through the psychic, Mel related that she would like to be remembered by her fun, joking, and joy, not by her Ataxia and the last few months of her life. I think she would approve of what Le chose. I can't believe it costs so much, good thing I'm still working. I've stayed home today to write out Mel's story and my concerns, so I can take it to the district attorney.

Journal Entry–October 31, 2004

Halloween–Mel's favorite holiday.

Mel "came" to my niece, Chelsea, shortly after her death. She said that although she didn't share my beliefs, she did believe in reincarnation. In reading her e-mail, she told someone that she gets feelings about people.

When we first moved into this house, Mel casually mentioned, "A man in black garb (Amish?) sits at the foot of my bed." This happened several times. After a while she told him to leave, that he frightens her. He did leave. I wonder if she tries to come to me or if she is angry with me? I wonder if we still have emotions when we pass?

I finally finished the package for the DA. Don will call this week to schedule a meeting after we return from our vacation. It was a relief to have it finished. Quite a relief!

We traveled to Western PA again to find either a house or land. We weren't successful.

Journal Entry–November 9, 2004

Don and I are in New Orleans, soon to board the Mississippi Queen for a river cruise up the Mississippi. Le and Morgen are staying in Erie while we are gone.

I called Le today to see how she was doing because she had a cold and has a history of breathing difficulties. I found out she was taken to the hospital this morning around 10:30 complaining that she couldn't breathe. It turns out she has a blood clot and is in intensive care. They have her on blood thinners and oxygen.

It's so hard to describe how I am feeling right now… it's like I'm deadened to any feeling…because if I do feel, it would be overload…too much. It seems that every time Don and I get away somebody in the family has a serious illness.

In the Jackson Square area in New Orleans, there are "readers" that set-up card tables along the sidewalks. I decided to obtain a psychic reading. The reader put emphasis in her speech as she related, "You are doing the right thing in regards to your daughter. What you start will change rules/laws on how things are done. It will have far-reaching results. Men up-to-the-age of 45 will be of help."

She foretold, "You will write a book and become famous because of it. You are a teacher and you need to get started." Shades of Twylah, huh? The reader continued, "You will know when it's time to write, and it will just come to you on how it should be laid out. All resources are in place to help you with the endeavor. More will be revealed as you go along."

Journal Entry–November 11, 2004

We awaken this morning, our first day on the Mississippi, to the sound of the ship's foghorn. There is nothing to see out our window except the pea soup dense fog.

Yesterday, Le was moved out of intensive care into the respiratory unit. She no longer needs oxygen. She was much worse than I was told. She has a blood clot in each lung. We will not be able to leave her alone even for a weekend. This came on so suddenly; it really is frightening. I'm glad we're moving to the Pittsburgh area so we have some family support.

Journal Entry–December 21, 2004

I find it very hard to sit down to write. It's as if writing is part of my grief and grief gets very heavy to carry in the conscious mind every day.

Every day I am conscious that Melanie is gone, or gone as I knew her. Her smile, I always see her Cheshire cat smile. Sometimes, I am sad and sometimes I am happy thinking she must be happy now. Sometimes, I thoroughly understand that it was not the life she wanted to live. That dreaded Ataxia took away her speech...her self-esteem...her body...and in the end...her soul. ATAXIA...ugh.

So much has happened this last month. Le'Anne weighs 89 ½ pounds. The doctor wants to insert a feeding tube into her stomach to provide some supplemental nourishment, to get some fat on her bones. If she should get sick again, she is not strong enough to ward it off. Le states she feels like a failure. She is embarrassed about it. It took her a week to make the decision. She has a consultation scheduled for December 30.

Work has not been going well. The director and the second in command (my supervisor) have been going head-to-head over me for several months. The woman who took over staff development came to me and said the director wants *me* to write a training program on disclosure of information. Wait a minute! Isn't this what she is supposed to be doing now? I asked my supervisor where this stood in my list of priorities and he said it didn't. A few days later, the director asked for a list of my assignments. I was told he has never been that interested in a lower-level employee before.

A few weeks later, the Human Resource Director called and said he wanted to talk to me about my job duties. What I am presently doing? How odd! Just a few months before, I was the Supervisor of Human Resources for our old Bureau so I knew the ropes. I asked if I was being downgraded. I wondered who wanted my higher-level pay grade position. Do they want to replace me with two lesser paid employees? I asked the Human Resource Director if he had talked to my supervisor about this. He replied, "No." Does my Bureau Director think that what he wants he will get, even if it disagrees with the State Office of Administration policies? A few days later, I was told there would be no desk audit.

Why was the bureau director out to get me? I wasn't causing any problems. Just the opposite, I was taking a lead role in the name of our bureau. I was on a statewide committee consisting of various state agencies including the Department of Corrections, the Community Colleges, and Department of Welfare. We were assigned the task of assessing the numerous vocational assessment instruments in use throughout the state to determine if we could refine the list to an agreed upon number that would be of benefit to all. This would eliminate multiple testing of a job seeker moving through the system that starts with determining appropriate training to actual job placement. I had done a lot of research and developed a chart comparing all the assessment tools currently in use and came up with a recommended list. The other agencies said it was very impressive and borrowed it for their own internal use.

Journal Entry–February 3, 2005

It's been a while since I've written. A lot has happened in this time span. I tell myself, I must sit down and write, but it takes discipline. And it reminds me of Melanie…

Le'Anne had the feeding tube inserted into her stomach. She is up to 101 pounds and is quite pleased. Everyone knows about the tube now; she wanted to keep it quiet for a while. Morgen accepts it as normal. They stayed with us for a few weeks after surgery.

These last weeks have brought many changes. I am no longer working. I took time off for Le's operation and decided I just couldn't go back to that hostile environment so I took family medical leave. I officially retire February 11th, 9 months before I have full retirement benefits. Because of this early retirement, I will receive no medical benefits from the state and will receive $175 a month less in cash benefits.

The job has not been "growing corn" as Gram would say, for the past year. The self-serving style of the new director didn't sit well with me. I was always for the good of the whole and he is for the good of promoting himself. It took the events brought about by my daughters to open my eyes to leave early. Leaving has taken away some of the stress in my life. I have worked for the state since 1982, since Mel was eleven months old. I must say, I don't miss it. Actually, it's a relief. I trust in the Universe to see to our financial needs. I also trust the Universe will take care of the director and his assistant… there is no need for me to harbor any revenge. What one puts out, eventually comes back around.

As of February 1st, our house is up for sale. It's kind of scary because we haven't found anything in Western PA yet. Again, I trust the Universe to send forth the right house for us.

Sooo…our new beginning has been set in motion…this next stage of our life has begun…it is the best of this lifetime…this I KNOW.

Journal Entry—February 9, 2005

Today is the Chinese New Year—the year of the rooster. I was born in 1945, another year of the rooster. It is really a new beginning, in many ways, a transition.

Today was my last session with the psychologist. I started seeing her to help me get through Melanie's death. Other than being a neutral person to talk with, I question how she helped. She is a lovely person who encouraged me that I was progressing. Is that her role? To make you aware of whether or not you are moving ahead?

If I had been asked this time last year to predict where I would be, it would not be anywhere close to this present reality. My life has completely changed!

Journal Entry—February 20, 2005

Le'Anne is in the hospital again, the third time since November. She has pneumonia. They moved her from a regular room into intensive care. After several tests, it was determined that she is inhaling food into her lungs and this is what is causing the pneumonia. She is not to take food or liquids by mouth for the rest of her life.

It was also determined that she does not have blood clots, she can stop taking blood thinners. In comparing the X-rays taken in Erie in November to the X-rays taken now, what appeared to be blood clots is actually scar tissue caused by the numerous bouts of pneumonia. Her lungs are filled with pockets of mucus throughout. The doctor thinks this will continue to happen because of the Ataxia. Her lungs are damaged. She can't afford any more damage. I can't afford to lose another daughter in such a short span. I don't know how I would come through another loss.

Blow it away Jean…it's not going to play out the way the doctors think. The Creator is working to help Le'Anne heal. This is my faith…the ones on the other side protect Morgen, and Morgen needs her mother.

Between Don and me taking care of Morgen and visiting Le in the hospital, there is no time left for other things. Finding land and building an appropriate house for all of us to live in is taking its toll on Don. At almost 82 years of age, it's just too much. Instead of him being taken care of, he has to help me with Le' and Morgen.

I am weak in spirit. All of this following on the heels of Melanie is a lot to withstand. I just pray for strength to get all of us through this. I worry about how many more years of quality of life Le has left. And I worry about Morgen's future; is she carrying that dreaded gene?

Journal Entry–March 5, 2005

Le has been out of the hospital for about two weeks. Although the doctor signed the papers, the nurse at the hospital was hesitant about releasing her at 5 PM. She thought Le was too weak to go home.

The two of us were nestled in my office/medicine room when the home health nurse arrived later that evening to teach us how to give Le's medications intravenously via a PICC line. This nurse was also concerned about Le's condition and left her personal phone number in case there was difficulty during the night.

After the nurse left, Le and I remained in my office going over the instructions when she started coughing and coughing and coughing. She brought up tons of mucus. This turned out to be the turning point in her recovery. Did the medication work that fast or was it my medicine objects that initiated this turn of events? After the coughing bout, she got a good night's sleep and the next day she felt and looked much better.

She is taking ten medicines that are delivered at various times throughout the day. Three are antibiotics; several are pills that are crushed and then dissolved in water to be put through her feeding tube; some are liquid, and one is given via the PICC line. First saline is pushed through the line, then the medication, followed by a flushing of saline. This continual vigilance reminds me of when she was a baby and nursed every two hours; there is little time for anything else. It puts wear and tear on Don and me. I thank the Creator that I have Don. I don't think I could have coped without his help. He is a Godsend.

I can't imagine what Le must be going through. It's got to be such a tremendous emotional and psychological reconciliation to not be able to eat food anymore. Our whole culture is built around food; all the holidays, birthdays, family, and civic celebrations have food at their center. She has such a passion for chocolate. Not being able to eat it anymore must be unbearable for her. I thank the Creator that she has Morgen to give her something to live for. Otherwise, I would be very concerned she might consider Melanie's route. She has so much to deal with, so much adjustment to make. She is such a lovely, strong soul!

All of us have been overwhelmed these past weeks. We have so much to do to bring Le back to a healthy status. She is still physically weak but has a strong constitution. I am so weary and so tired, but this doesn't compare to what Le is going through.

Journal Entry–April 30, 2005

Tomorrow night it will be ten months since Melanie decided to leave us. It still seems so surreal. I think of her every day and send her my love. It's as if she is living somewhere else, far away where she can't come to visit. I can't think of her as being totally gone. Love doesn't die. If only she could have felt love…things may have evolved differently.

I received a reading from another intuitive counselor in Lilly Dale. She states, "Mel came into this life to examine unconditional love. In her death, she realized she *was* loved. You should feel joy that she experienced what she came to experience, that she learned her life lesson. You two have been together before. She knew you would help her in this lesson."

I have written earlier about Mel being sick around five or six years of age and how I thought another soul might have entered her body. I finally asked Spirit about this. I was told, "You are correct. Another did come in, but that it was a different aspect of Melanie's soul. The aspect that left could not handle what was to come in her life." Well, it seems this aspect of Melanie couldn't handle it either!

Both of my girls were dealt difficult hands. It's a wonder we all aren't loony. I know my memory has suffered greatly this last year.

I honestly don't know how I could have proven my love for Melanie more. She was always emotional needy. No matter how much I gave, it wasn't enough. She didn't know how to exist on her own. I tried to help her become independent, but she wanted to be taken care of like when she was little.

It was decided that Le and Morgen would move back in with us permanently. They had to be out of the apartment by March 30. Because of conflicting schedules, the only weekend my sisters could help us move Le's things into storage was the weekend of March 20…Mel's birthday. I really wanted all my children to be together at the gravesite to celebrate her birthday, but it was not to be.

I'm so glad that Ed and his family were able to go to the cemetery. When we went to visit Ed for Easter, his daughter Ally said to me in a soft whisper, "Melanie is dead, isn't she?" We always told the grandchildren that she became an angel, but didn't elaborate on how. On Easter morning I cried thinking how much Mel enjoyed the annual Easter egg hunt, how she always hid the eggs.

We found a house and will close on July 20. I wanted to be out of this house before July 1st. I can't stand the thought of living here during that time. Don is taking me to Massachusetts for a long July 4th weekend so we will at least be away.

Journal Entry–May 20, 2005

We got home a few days ago from spending a week with Don's daughter in Seattle. The grieving process is so unpredictable. We were visiting Leavenworth, a quaint little Bavarian Village nestled in the central Cascade Mountains of Washington State. Don's grandson is to be married there in June 2006. A May Day celebration was in progress; we were enjoying a school chorus singing swing songs. I was commenting on how some of the kids were really into it when all of a sudden a torrent of tears broke loose. I was overwhelmed with the loss of Melanie. She was in the school chorus for six years and I attended all her concerts.

Now that things are calming down, more emotions are popping up. The first several months I was numb; then all hell broke loose with Le'Anne's health. I keep seeing Melanie standing there with the knife in her hand and lying on the floor where she dropped, knowing it was my words that must have been the final straw for her. Will I ever be able to forgive myself?

Journal Entry–May 23, 2005

Tonight, the Larry King show was about near death experiences, how the will to live was stronger than the circumstances leading to death. All the guests talked about how their lives have changed for the better, how they didn't have time/patience for complainers. How they wanted to shake these types of people and make them aware of just how precious life is.

A woman called in talking about how she too had almost lost her life and was still suffering from the "why me" syndrome. She was advised by the guests on the show to obtain some counseling. She was also advised to reach out to others in need, that helping others will help her to heal, to get outside of herself, that she has something to share.

It is nearing the one-year anniversary of Melanie's passing. Now that all the crises appear to be over, I have some downtime for reflection. Le'Anne is doing well and has regained her weight. Her complexion now glows with the perfect nutrition of her liquid diet. She doesn't seem to mind that she cannot eat; instead, she now smells the foods she once enjoyed. She said, "It beats being sick all the time." I do think of Melanie everyday and send her prayers for her well-being. Some days, I get into a funk when I think about what has happened to my family. I have always been told that I must share my knowledge. *She Who Knows*, knows that in order to heal completely, I must get outside myself. In the past, I have done a few spiritual workshops that were warmly received. It is time to begin…to share my experiences…what I have learned the hard way… and to trust that it will lighten someone else's load. I would not wish this past year on anyone.

Journal Entry–July 5, 2005

Don and I returned home today from spending five days in Massachusetts. We left on Thursday morning so I wouldn't be in the house on July 1ˢᵗ. I didn't want to celebrate Melanie's death…nor did I want to be in the house on that day…too many painful memories to endure. The night of July 1ˢᵗ, I took some sleeping pills. I didn't want to be awake at the time Mel left us. We will move into our new house at the end of this month. A new beginning.

Journal Entry–July 25, 2005

Moving day, but there is one piece of unfinished business I must do. I talked to my friend Susan last week and said I wanted to go to Justin's house. She said, "There is much more to this then what he knows. Send the book you compiled (the DA office was not interested) to the local police and give them your new address. Something will come up and they will get in touch with you." She continued, "These people and their bad energy cannot stay hidden forever. You will get your answers in time."

While the packers were at work, Don and I took the binder to the Lower Paxton Police Department and with tears in my eyes, I handed it over to the head of the detectives. He mumbled something about not really knowing our children; a friend of his had a similar experience and they found out afterwards that their son was on drugs. I tersely replied, "The autopsy revealed there were no drugs in her body." Then I turned to leave. Why do the police look at the age of the deceased and, if young, always think it has to do with drugs?

Chapter 20

Journal Entry–May 19, 2006, 2:20 PM

Playing a mindless computer card game is my way of occupying time until Twylah arrives. It's been many years since we have seen each other. Too many.

We've rearranged the house to accommodate an elderly grandma who is no longer able to skillfully negotiate stairs. Le'Anne moved upstairs to the guest room and Twylah will stay in Le's bedroom on the main floor. My family doesn't know what to expect; after all, Gram is ninety-three years old. We can't guesstimate how much of our time and energy will be needed to make Twy's visit comfortable.

How did this fantastic opportunity come about? Serendipity? I was working on the first draft of this book and had asked both Melanie and Twylah to give me a sign showing consent; I didn't want to go forward if they objected; after all, it's their story also. That night they appeared together in a dream. They were wearing wide grins and had their arms and hands interlocked in a loving bond as if to say, "We are in this together, with you, all the way." Gram's eyes and lips showed the same smitten smile she wore upon my return from Texas. Mel wore her Cheshire cat grin.

Upon awakening I was somewhat torn on how to interpret the dream. Had Gram passed over; were they now together on the other side? Mel had never really embraced my spiritual beliefs. Did this dream mean that upon meeting Gram in spirit, Mel could now recognize the value of the teachings? I decided to elicit my friend Susan's take on this.

I called Susan and posed the question. She paused for a second and then began, "Gram has not passed; I would know if she has, I would feel it inside and I don't get that feeling." I felt relieved, as I thought I would also know when Gram passes. After all, Gram said we are cut from the same cloth.

Susan continued, "I think your interpretation of their approval is correct. Wow, Jean, what a powerful affirmation!"

Gram's son and his wife were traveling to England, Germany, and Holland for seven weeks to share the teachings with others of like mind. They phoned from out of the blue and asked if I would come down to Florida to take care of Twylah for one of the weeks they were to be away as Twy is no longer able to travel for long periods of time. I stated that if she were able to come to my house, I would keep her the whole time.

On hanging up, meandering thoughts snaked through my mind. Is Twy making her good-byes to those who have truly embraced her teachings? Will she pass shortly after our visit? Susan had the same thoughts. Susan thinks Gram has something to pass on to me before she leaves this Earthplane.

I started to get butterflies with the anticipation of Gram's arrival. Finally, their car appeared in the driveway. I couldn't wait for them to get out...I ran through the garage to greet them. I pressed my face to the glass of the back window and observed Gram's small fragile frame postured behind the safety of her seat belt. As she released the latch, a flash of relief spread across her face as she realized the long ride was finally over. Her face lit-up with recognition as I opened the door to welcome her.

After a half-hour, her son and his wife said farewell and left us with a binder of instructions for Twy's care and emergency numbers just in case. Their parting words were, "We'll call periodically to check in with her and to answer any questions you may have on her care." So began one of the most significant two weeks of my life.

Journal Entry-May 19, 2006, continued...10:16 PM

Gram arrived around 3 PM. We were all so excited we stayed up until ten o'clock talking our heads off. Twy had us all howling when she confessed that she was called Turd Hurd in school.

After things settled down, we talked a bit about a few of my spiritual adventures. I related an interesting experience I had when Don and I were on an Alaskan cruise. The morning we were to sail into Sitka, an Elder of the Tlingit Nation came aboard and told us a story surrounding a "Messenger Doll" housed in a Native American Museum in Sitka, Alaska. Upon setting foot on land, I headed towards the museum to see if I could intuitively pick out that particular doll from the rest in the case. Although my eyes kept going to a large red painted statue in the corner on the lowest shelf, I felt this was too big to be called a "doll." Giving up, I asked the docent to show me. Sure enough, the big red one in the corner was the "Messenger Doll." Gram confirmed that in a spiritual context, I did what I was supposed to do. I'm positive that doll passed on a message to me. However, on a conscious level, I have no idea what it is.

I then proceeded to tell her about the two separate encounters when Susan and I were stopped on the streets in Glastonbury, England. Both times, we were asked if we had been to the Chalice Well. I knew if something came before you twice, it was a message from Spirit. Although we had been to the top of the Tor, we hadn't seen the well. Susan just couldn't absorb anymore for the day, she was already on spiritual overload from what had taken place earlier. Gram acknowledged what I already knew, that we had missed a spiritual opportunity.

Journal Entry–May 20, 2006

Twylah's inner knowing revealed: Morgen didn't know if she wanted to come in as a boy or a girl. People will be drawn towards her. Be careful she doesn't get in with the wrong crowd. There is more to Melanie's death that will be revealed at the "right time." Things will start to leak out. Somebody is being paid off to keep quiet.

My family said it was such a pleasure to have Twylah in our house. She was a joy to be around. Le' Anne was so happy to see Gram again as Le had accompanied me to the reservation many times. After Gram left, Morgen would often say, "I miss Grandma Twylah. She would sit by me on the couch and talk and play with me. I love her."

Don was pleased to reveal, "Twylah is nothing like I anticipated. She's quite capable of tending to her own needs." He delighted in their conversations. Gram spoke to him about the teachings, and he felt honored that she would take the time to help him learn his "colors." When they were finished, he exclaimed, "She was right on!" He genially remembers how she flirted outrageously with him and how he loved every minute of it. Both sets of eyes sparkled immensely during these mutual exchanges!

In our active household there is always something going on. Don and I were to attend a pops concert in Pittsburgh. My sister, Sylvia, had consented to stay with Twy for the few hours we would be gone. She said, "I'd like to come up beforehand so I'll know what I'm getting myself into." After a brief visit, she left saying, "Boy, am I pleasantly surprised! Twylah is not what I expected. What a sense of humor she has! I look forward to spending time with her."

It was one of those beautiful spring mornings. The rising sun peeked through the window to find Gram and me alone at the kitchen table after breakfast. Gram started talking about the Pathway of Peace. It had been a long time and I wasn't sure I could accurately remember the traditional placement of each color so I pulled out my old workbook from years ago. I remember when she told me there was something on my truth line I was not using. Now as she reviewed my chart she disclosed, "Geez, you have a hard truth line, it's at odds with each other."

The truth line runs from the 12 o'clock position (north) to the 6 o'clock position (south). My personal colors representing these positions are black and blue. All of a sudden, it hit me what this placement meant. Surprised, I relayed to Gram, "I can now understand what this means. I have great intuition (blue) if I listen within (black). Unfortunately, if somebody questions my actions or states I am wrong I usually back down, believing them before myself. I have little confidence in what I *know* although the passage of time usually proves me correct. Instead of listening within, I listen to others. I guess I spiritually beat myself up until I'm black and blue! I must learn to listen to myself." Gram looked into my eyes and with a smile replied, "Good, now you know what you must do."

My son, Ed, and his family came for dinner one Sunday. We were all sitting around the dining room table after dinner when Gram proceeded to make the parents aware of how the personalities of each child would play out in the future. She had us all in stitches as she had tagged each one correctly. She continued with, "The one you will really have to watch out for is this one here." Madison is not only the youngest, but also the quietest of my grandchildren. I call her the Happy Buddha because she doesn't say much but her knowing smile says it all. Gram continued, "Look into her eyes, they tell the whole story." Ed and Cris laughed as they said, "Yes, we think we'll have our hands full!"

Gram loved having people around. She even had the window cleaner, Mark, eating out of her hand. Each morning Twy would ask, "What's in store for today? Who's coming?" She seemed disappointed when I would say, "Nobody today, Gram."

It was a quiet afternoon with just the two of us left at the lunch table. Twylah thought out loud, "I wonder if it was worth the sacrifice? All the writing I did? Is anybody paying attention anymore? Are they listening?" To ward off her self-doubt, I assured her they were, that's why her son was in Europe, that's why I'm writing the book…so the teachings may live.

I explained how I wanted to carry on the teachings through writing children's books. The main character is to be called Grandmother Twylah. Gram empathically told me not to do that. She explained, "They are your writings, not mine. They should carry your name; you need to take ownership of what you write."

A little later that day, I related the circumstances surrounding Melanie's death to Twylah and told her of my suspicions. She confirmed my thoughts by saying, "Jean, you are right. There is more to this. It will come out in the fullness of time. They can't hide forever."

Don and I had plans in place to attend his grandson's wedding in Washington State scheduled for early June. Susan was to stay with Gram while we were away. She came a few days early so the three of us could visit together as we had done so many times before at Gram's house.

Out of the three of us, Susan is the quietest; she likes to keep things simple. She prefers to experience one event and digest it before moving on. I, on the other hand, tend to go full steam, taking in everything I possibly can. Later, I will fully reflect on the events to discern their impact.

Every evening after dinner and before Morgen's bedtime, we had an hour of downtime. During this hour Susan, Gram, and I would sit in wooden rockers on the front porch and watch my neighbor land his ultra-light after soaring over the surrounding swells of land. The ultra-light resembled a go-cart attached to a multi-colored parachute. Although it was hard for Gram to see that far, she could pick out the bright colors of the sail. She exclaimed, "How does that thing fly?"

Twy loved relaxing in the rockers. She would sigh, "How peaceful it is here, this land is so beautiful; this is a good place to be." I never knew if she meant the piece of land was a good place to be or our home; perhaps she meant both. As we rocked away the hour, we discussed the varieties of birds that darted in and out of the bushes lining the perimeter of the porch.

We watched as the twilight sky slowly changed into its evening colors and enjoyed the companionable patches of silence as we sat relaxed, rested, and reposed.

Gram especially liked this time of the evening. Her eyes lit-up as she asked, "What's for dessert tonight?" Susan would disappear into the house and reemerge with three bowls of ice cream. As she glanced into the bowl intended for Gram, she said, "Whoops, I think I put too much in this bowl!" Gram gazed into the bowl and with a twinkle in her eyes replied, "I don't think so; I can handle that!"

Our house sits in an old cow pasture on three acres of horse-fenced land. I explained to Gram that I wanted to plant a circle of pines medicine wheel in the backyard; like the circle she had planted on her land so many years ago. Gram was delighted and proceeded to explain how it should be carried out. Even though Gram has stopped presenting the teachings, she remains the teacher. She can't help being who she is. Her body may be aging, but she still possesses a strong spirit.

Susan, Gram, and I laughed like schoolgirls as we shared our memories of the various events that took place on Gram's land. After a few minutes, I asked Gram, "Do you want to hear something really funny? Well, I had a dream that Susan and I are to conduct a secret spiritual mission." After explaining the assignment, I expected Gram to say, "Well, that was quite a dream!" Instead she pierced my very being with her dark penetrating eyes and then inquired, "You know how to do it, don't you?" With a twinkle in her eye, she looked from me to Susan and back waiting for a response. She wasn't going to give us the answer easily; she was testing us as she had done so many times in the past. After we had given a few incorrect responses, I gave up and throwing my hands into the air declared, "I haven't the foggiest!" Susan nodded in agreement. Gram chuckled as she gave us precise instructions. Susan and I howled at what we are to do. Gram joined in and there were tears in our eyes from all the amusement. Will it turn out to be that easy?

Gram believes that dreams are messages from the Creator and are not to be ignored. Years ago, I can remember her saying, "Jean, you are standing in the portal, why won't you step through?" Now, her knowing smile revealed that I had finally cracked open a doorway Susan and I had always suspected Gram had entry to; a portal that leads to a deeper spiritual level. Long ago, we recognized that Twylah's simple lessons on life contained a deeper mystery.

Living the teachings provided entrance to other levels of understanding. My dream was Twylah's validation that her "other work" would also be carried on.

She seemed quite pleased that she could fully retire, that the torch had been passed. The care keepers are leaving the Earthplane and passing on their duties to those who hear the call. Earlier in our conversation, Twy had stated that she knew her son would continue her teachings set in the Seneca tradition; that this was his inheritance.

The next day as Don and I were packing for our trip to Washington, the phone rang. We were asked to pack Twylah's belongings, as her daughter would be arriving to take Twylah to her house until Bob's return.

As I walked Gram to the door for the last time, she took me aside and quietly instructed, "Now listen Jean, you know your mission in life. Don't let anything or anybody stop you or keep you from it." As we shuffled towards the car, she took Susan aside to whisper final instructions to her.

There were kisses and hugs all around, and then the car pulled away with Twylah in the back seat, once again tucked behind the safety of her seat belt. There was finality to her parting. The feeling hung heavy in the air. We all had tears in our eyes. Two weeks were all we had, but it was enough.

Unknown to me at the time, a spiritual circle was in final approach for its 360-degree turn. It is now me putting out the call to Twylah. It is now my kitchen table we sit around. It is now my time to be a teacher. I can no longer say, "Not now." Twylah has stepped down…I must step up.

o o o o o

If real life were like the movies, this is the spot where I would be tying up all the loose ends to bring about resolution. But it isn't…and I can't. There isn't a neat package to be wrapped. In my journey to seek the truth of Melanie's death, I had to take a journey within myself. If I didn't understand and accept what was inside of me, how could I understand anything else?

We all come to that fatal instant moment…when something bad happens…and we can't turn back the clock. Right after Melanie's death, I wanted the answers to everything. Now I respect the fact that I can't have all the answers.

I learned through the teachings of Twylah Nitsch how to become spiritually prepared for the storms that come my way. She taught me how to charge my battery for those times when I have to go the extra mile. Knowing the Creator's love is within all of us has brought comfort during the tempest and produced the *Afterglow*.

When one doesn't accept their self-worth, they tend to experience the world with an egotistical view. They are fearful that others will see them as lacking. Twylah's teachings lead to self-acceptance and a sense of self-worth. This leads to being more accepting of others because we are more accepting of ourselves.

In retrospect, I can understand why I was attracted to the nature based Native American way of healing. As a child, I was instinctively drawn to Mother Nature. She comforted my soul and dried my tears. I walked in her flowered woods and sat under her stately shady trees. I still visit the trees of my youth and thank them for their help. My granddaughter, Morgen, has found a tree friend near my father's grave which is located in the cemetery I played in as a child. Morgen asks, "When we can go back to visit my friend?"

In the years that have passed since Melanie's passing, I have learned that grief changes shape. I have learned that it *can* be transformed and instead of feeling pain and confusion, we are together in memory; there is solace and pleasure there, not just loss. Life is precious. It *is* worthwhile.

Through Melanie, I now realize that to understand the human condition is to know that we all want to find inner peace and contentment; that the greatest form of love is to allow the consequences that accrue from another's own free will. It is one thing to understand this intellectually; to absorb it emotionally is another. THIS I KNOW.

I also know that after loss, there comes a point when life must be reclaimed. You have to reject being overwhelmed. Life must go on. A point is reached where you don't want to flee from life anymore. I know the heartache of life...I also know the beauty of it.

The seers say we identify ourselves too much with our physical bodies. We must remember that we are a soul having a physical experience, not a physical being whose soul dies upon death. Mel may no longer be here in body, but she is with me in spirit. I can now read her signs and feel her love once again. Love is the force that transforms and improves; it makes us strive to become better.

I had reached a point in the book where I was stuck and asked Mel to help write her point of view. Suddenly, Morgen came running in from outside.

Wearing her perpetual dirty face she called out, "Look Grandma, see what I have for you. No, it's for the whole family." It was a stalk of daisies, complete with roots and dirt.

In high school, Mel's inner circle of girlfriends took to calling themselves names of flowers, after the little dolls dressed up as flowers that were so popular back then. Guess what Mel's name was? Yup, Daisy! I interpreted Morgen's flower delivery as a physical reminder that Melanie was with me. The roots and dirt were removed so the flowers could be placed on the top of my computer monitor where they were within sight. Shortly after, I got the inspiration to include Mel's e-mails in the book, her point of view. If it were not for Gram's teachings of learning how to accept guidance from all of nature, the message from the daisies would not have been realized.

Later in the week, my husband was sitting at his computer when he noticed an inactive program on the task bar at the bottom of the screen. When he clicked on it, a picture of two dolphins appeared. He said out loud, "Hi Melanie." Later, when relating the story to me, Don said he had no idea where the picture came from; that it was not in any program or e-mail, it just appeared out of nowhere. There are no coincidences in life.

o o o o o

I share my story with you as a way to help others to accept their worthiness and mission in life. My wish for you, dear reader, is that you recognize that you possess the faith and courage to pursue your personal spiritual mission, that mysterious magnet of destiny that is obscured by countless distractions and obstacles. Learn to trust your heart, to read the subtle signs, and to understand that as *you* look to fulfill a dream, it looks to fulfill *you*. To realize your mission in life is your spiritual obligation. The entire universe is at your disposal.

When we know who we are, we know the joys and sorrows of ourselves. When we fully accept our polarity is when we can move on. *Afterglow* occurs when the cup of sorrow is empty.

Good journeys.

With gratitude,

She Who Knows

Epilogue

As I sat down to write this book, I said a prayer and asked both Melanie and Grandmother Twylah Nitsch to give me some kind of a sign that it was all right to go ahead with the book. After all, it was their story as well as mine. A few nights later I had the following dream: Mel and Gram were standing with their arms intertwined in front of them, holding each other's hands as if linked together in a shared intent. Mel wore her big Cheshire cat grin and Gram was gazing at me with her sparkling eyes and smitten smile, the same way she looked at me when I returned from Texas. It was as if she were saying, "Way to go Jean, I knew you could do it!"

I will remember this dream always. It's the only time Melanie has appeared to me. I was elated to find her happy and thriving. How grateful I was to see them happy together and approving of the book.

I don't think I could have made it through Melanie's passing if not for Twylah's teachings. They gave me a solid foundation for how I want to live my life. She taught that the Creator gave us freedom of choice. I can choose to suffer in despair for the rest of my years or I can use the experience to help others. I choose the latter.

I can't say if it was her pen and paper exercises or being in her presence that made me want to be a better person...to help others in this lesson called life...to heal myself so I can help lead the way and demonstrate how others can heal also. We all contain the energy of our maker...the Creator...as does the trees, the rocks, the water, and the creature teachers. How could we not... if he made us all? All for One...One for All.

Twylah dropped her robes (died) in August 2007. Like Melanie, she is always with me in spirit. Gram said she would always sit in the center of our group. There will always be Susan, Janet, Twylah and myself. Others will come and go, but the four of us remain spiritually linked.

We are now in the fifth world and will fully transition by the year 2013. The fourth world was about separation, separation of the Earth into different continents, separation of people by color and language. It was a world of power and control. The fifth world is about unity and illumination. Those people who were in control are now finding they cannot hold onto something they never had. Control is just an illusion.

Another event took place in the last half of 2007 that brought me no surprise. Through the grapevine, I learned the bureau director was fired. The politically correct statement issued stated that he retired. It's my understanding that the Capitol Police escorted him out of the building, his computer was confiscated, and his office put under lock and key. What's so amazing is it wasn't the number of women who supposedly had filed sexual harassment charges against him that finally brought him down, but a meek, mild mannered man who just wanted to do his job. This is the way life plays out; it was no macho showdown, just a quiet man who stood his ground…in Truth. Gram always said that if you stand in your Truth nobody could hurt you. A few months later, the executive assistant left for a small nondescript agency.

I look forward to being fully in the fifth world…a world where people from all walks of life will unite for the good of the whole. This will raise the vibration rate of Earth and illuminate our galaxy in this great vastness called space. As we heal…so does Mother Earth. We are all in this dream together. Each of us is a piece of the puzzle. Each of us can help the other to progress in becoming whole to complete the puzzle. Not one person is more important than the other. We each have something to share. This is why I tell my story.

Einstein offered the following to a person who was grieving over the loss of his son and was looking for some consolation:

"A human being is part of the whole, called by us 'Universe,' a part limited in time and space. He experiences himself, his thoughts, and feelings, as something separated from the rest—a kind of optical delusion of his consciousness. This delusion is a kind of prison for us, restricting us to our desires and to affections for a few persons nearest to us. Our task must be to free ourselves from this prison by widening our circle of compassion to embrace all living creatures and the whole of nature in its beauty."

Albert Einstein